"This modern classic relishes in collapsing conventional and clichéd orthodoxies. As formative as Harrison's proclamations are, it is Harrison's pacing that gives the book the lingering feeling of the most sensual whisper."

—**KIESE LAYMON,** author of
Heavy: An American Memoir

"*Belly of the Beast* is written with poise and lucidity. It pushes us to think past the pablum of telling fat folx all they gotta do is love themselves to enacting a movement that addresses the source and ramifications of societal anti-fatness as anti-Blackness. Harrison forces us not to look away, reminding us that all too often 'health' and 'desire' are used to annul Blackness. In a 'post bo-po' world, desire and the sheer right to life can be rooted in something other than all the things named non-Black."

—**SABRINA STRINGS,** author of *Fearing the Black Body: The Racial Origins of Fat Phobia*

"Da'Shaun Harrison is an insightful visionary, world-builder, and ingenious writer who brings us into deeper understandings and frameworks of the intersections of anti-Blackness and anti-fatness. *Belly of the Beast* brings us closer to ourselves because it brings us closer to the truth—that anti-Blackness is the foundation to how violence shapes our relationships to our bodies and each other. Harrison not only intervenes in the terror of white supremacist paradigms but develops the tools to imagine and build a new world. *Belly of the Beast* eats, and it leaves no crumbs."

—**HUNTER SHACKELFORD,** author of *You Might Die for This*

"I am continually blown away by Da'Shaun's ability as a writer to wrestle so deeply and expertly with questions many of us would never even think to ask—whether they be about our world, our politics, our selves, or our bodies. Every page challenges us to expand our imagination and reconstruct the ways we think, talk, and theorize about fatness, Blackness, gender, health, desire, abolition, and more. *Belly of the Beast* is a gift and a groundbreaker."

—**SHERRONDA J. BROWN,** editor-in-chief of *Wear Your Voice* magazine

BELLY OF THE BEAST

THE POLITICS OF ANTI-FATNESS AS ANTI-BLACKNESS

Da'Shaun L. Harrison

Foreword by Kiese Laymon

North Atlantic Books
Berkeley, California

Published by
North Atlantic Books
Huichin, unceded Ohlone land
aka Berkeley, California

Cover photo by Da'Shaun L. Harrison
Cover design by Sherronda J. Brown
Book design by Happenstance Type-O-Rama

Printed in the United States of America

Belly of the Beast: The Politics of Anti-Fatness as Anti-Blackness is sponsored and published by North Atlantic Books, an educational nonprofit based in the unceded Ohlone land Huichin (*aka* Berkeley, CA) that collaborates with partners to develop cross-cultural perspectives; nurture holistic views of art, science, the humanities, and healing; and seed personal and global transformation by publishing work on the relationship of body, spirit, and nature.

North Atlantic Books' publications are distributed to the US trade and internationally by Penguin Random House Publisher Services. For further information, visit our website at www.northatlanticbooks.com.

Library of Congress Cataloging-in-Publication Data
Names: Harrison, Da'Shaun, 1996– author.
Title: Belly of the beast : the politics of anti-fatness as anti-blackness / Da'Shaun Harrison.
Description: Berkeley, CA : North Atlantic Books, [2021] | Includes bibliographical references and index. | Summary: "An exploration of anti-fatness and anti-Blackness at the intersections of race, police violence, gender identity, fatness, and health"— Provided by publisher.
Identifiers: LCCN 2020055026 (print) | LCCN 2020055027 (ebook) | ISBN 9781623175979 (trade paperback) | ISBN 9781623175986 (ebook)
Subjects: LCSH: African American men—Social conditions. | Obesity in men—Social aspects—United States. | Overweight men—United States—Social conditions. | Body image—Social aspects—United States. | Masculinity—United States. | African American men—Violence against.
Classification: LCC E185.86 .H376 2021 (print) | LCC E185.86 (ebook) | DDC 305.38/896073—dc23
LC record available at https://lccn.loc.gov/2020055026
LC ebook record available at https://lccn.loc.gov/2020055027

3 4 5 6 7 8 9 KPC 26 25 24 23 22

North Atlantic Books is committed to the protection of our environment. We print on recycled paper whenever possible and partner with printers who strive to use environmentally responsible practices.

CONTENTS

FOREWORD

I am a fat Black and I would like to help Da'Shaun Harrison destroy the worlds.

That sentence defines me more profoundly than my name or any of my art. There will be plenty books and essays written about what Harrison has done with *Belly of the Beast: The Politics of Anti-Fatness as Anti-Blackness*. Many will wonder about the rhetorical dexterity necessary to pull off such generative, and really luscious, theorizing. Folks will write about how Harrison welcomes us into the mushy procreant spaces beyond self-love, beyond health, beyond desirability, beyond human, beyond gender, and beyond abolition. Readers will talk about how Harrison names what is on the other side of, and within, all of these designations, as they invite us into the glorious stank act of radical revision (which is always a razing and generative act—even if ephemeral). Most will remember the book's tenderness, its pleasurable rigor and its fat Black plea to demolish normal as we know it.

But. I want to talk about fantasy. *And.* I want to talk about fantasy.

Like a lot of you, I have tried to choke, and eventually been choked out by, disordered eating, exercise obsession, and body dysmorphia. I'm not sure anyone raised in this nation actually has a radically loving relationship with their body, their mirror, or their food, but I am "healthier" than I've ever been, and I am still never in my sexual fantasies or my sexual memories. I write and read to find my Black body, my Black body parts, both yesterday and tomorrow's Black collective body. But what does it actually mean to find our fat Black bodies in our fantasies? How do conventional understandings of time, place, pleasure, and consent build worlds in our fat Black bodies? How do we begin the work of world-building and world-obliteration off the page?

Belly of the Beast carried me to question why, in my fantasies, I am always far more traditionally masculine, and far less traditionally femme than I am in "real" space and time. In my memory, the ones I choose not to run from, I long not to be that same uber-masculine clone of myself. I want to be soft. I want to accept that the women in my fantasies might love and/or desire my softness? The women and genderqueer folk I meet in my fantasies and my memory have far more elasticity than the version of me I create there. But they are not nearly as elastic in body and character as the women with whom I am actually attracted? So while I am a completely distorted version of myself in my fantasies, the women in my fantasies are always women I've loved in the past. This means that in addition to creating a less fat, Black loving version of myself in my fantasies, I'm also only imagining love and sex with younger versions of myself and my partner. I'm erasing myself at a time in my life when I most need to be present.

Harrison has convinced me that this isn't something to write off, or something to simply write down and to pat myself on the back for acknowledging. Our fantasies, like *our* utopias, don't just say everything about who we are; they define where we are, and in defining what we are, they dictate what, and how, we will love, organize, fight, win, and lose. Heterotopias are real. And fake. They live in our fat Black bodies. And they do not live at all. This is, perhaps, the most triumphant revelation in *Belly of the Beast*. The fat Black folks we love are the world. The fat Black folks who love us are the world. Those fat Black folks, responsible for the most abundant and trifling parts of us, are worthy of the most exquisite destruction. And we are worthy of being tenderly destroyed by them.

As a fat Black boy artist who was always afraid of being seen, this modern classic relishes in collapsing conventional and clichéd orthodoxies. As formative as Harrison's proclamations are, it is Harrison's pacing that gives the book the lingering feeling of the most sensual whisper. *Belly of the Beast* took me behind what I've been told is liberation and said, "I want to destroy the world that manufactures and houses the cage by which the fat Black is bound."

I am a fat Black and I'd like to help Da'Shaun Harrison destroy our worlds. I know you will, too.

KIESE LAYMON,
author of *Heavy: An American Memoir*

ACKNOWLEDGMENTS

I n *Are Prisons Obsolete?*, Angela Y. Davis starts her acknowledgments off by saying, "I should not be listed as the sole author of this book, for its ideas reflect various forms of collaboration over the last six years with activists, scholars, prisoners, and cultural workers . . ." Similar to her, I have come across and been in conversation with many people over the last seven years—and beyond—who have made this moment possible. I would have to write another book to list all the names of everyone who has journeyed with me, and perhaps one day I will, but for now I will do my best to list everyone I can within the confines of the space I have.

To Nichelle Spicer-Watkins, who I'm lucky to affectionately call Mama, thank you. If not for your labor, your love, and your labor of love, this would not have been possible. To my nana, Fran Spicer-Whitehead, and my aunts, Kimberly Spicer and Sonya Evans, thank you. If not for your ability and willingness to care for Mama when she went above and beyond to care for me, this would not have been possible. Thank you to my self-proclaimed managers, my brothers, Da'Quan and Cedric Harrison, for the laughs, the love, and the headaches. A thank you to my stepdad, Joey "Big Joe" Watkins, and my

cnt_333.3. 333.33

step-grandfather, Steve Whitehead, for the same. To the rest of my family, immediate and otherwise, I thank you.

A special thank you to my queer parent, Hunter Shackelford, for holding me with so much love, grace, and care. I love better because of you. Thank you to one of my best friends, Jordan Mulkey, for all of the knowledge you've imparted into me; for the countless days and sleepless nights that we laughed and thought together. A huge thank you to my other best friends, Delaney Vandergrift and Terrance McQueen, for whom I am forever grateful. You have both loved me in ways unimaginable. To Justin James and Antoinette Kelley, I am forever thankful for and to you for seeing something special in me that you selflessly nurtured and helped grow. To the rest of my chosen family: Jaylen Thomas, Raekwon and Taekwon Griffin, Maurice Brooks, Fredric Wood, Jaeden Johnson, and Damani Warren, thank you for loving me so dearly—all the laughs, late night rendezvous, and endless support have pushed me to this exact moment. Thank you to the community of people who have held me down and held me close; who have crossed oceans and climbed mountains on my behalf: Simi Moonlight, Tea Troutman, RAW, Jill Cartwright, Eva Dickerson, Aurielle Marie, Desi Hall, and August Clayton. Thank you, Josh, Kings, and Q for holding me, challenging me, and loving me. And thank you Daviava, Nathanael, and Shydeik. For all of you, my love is endless.

Thank you to Avery Jackson. Your endless work introduced me to a world I otherwise would have never known and a strength I would have otherwise abandoned. To Dr. Natasha Walker, thank you for being the first to believe in me. Without your encouragement, your guidance, your friendship, and your mentorship, this book would have never been written. I love you forever. Dr. Daniel Black, thank you for teaching me to dream bigger, to read more intently, and to write more concisely. Your impact on my life and my life's work is immeasurable. A special thank you to Lara Witt and Sherronda J. Brown for giving me the opportunity to write what I dream and for unlocking new dreams for me to write about.

On my journey to this moment, there were editors I worked with who impacted me, the way I think, and the way I write in more ways than they know—two of them being Hari Ziyad and Arielle Newton. Thank you both for believing in my work and for trusting me to write with so much care about Black people.

A very big and very special thank you to Kiese Laymon for all of the support you've shown me throughout this entire process. I am so honored to witness your brilliance in real time, family. Thank you to Sabrina Strings for all of your continued kindness; it means the world to me.

Thank you to Caleb Luna, Becca, and everyone else who offered feedback on this project. And to every fat person with whom I have existed in community for years—digital and otherwise. That list is very long, but I specifically want to name and thank Aubrey Gordon and Sofie Hagen who were both gracious enough to acknowledge me in their brilliant works. Thank you also to Sydneysky G. Your work and your friendship have had a continued impact on my work and how I theorize around our lives. I am so thankful for you.

Thank you to all of my Spelhouse friends and siblings. Thank you to all of my Twitter followers who have journeyed along with me, from start to finish.

A huge thank you to my editor, Shayna Keyles, for making all of this happen. You saw and embraced my vision from the beginning and helped to actualize it with so much care and effort. I am so grateful. And to all of the rest of the North Atlantic Books family, thank you.

To every friend, every stranger, every acquaintance, every community member—to everyone who has ever supported me, uplifted me, poured into me, or otherwise helped me make it to this point, thank you. I am so grateful for the ways each of you have contributed to my life.

And finally, thank you to all of the fat Black folks around the globe for whom I write with great diligence and intention. All of you helped write this book, too. All of the brilliant fat Black folks producing brilliant content online, who may never get to see their names on the cover of a book, this book is for you too.

1

Beyond Self-Love

In this book, we will talk about the body. Not just any body, but the fat Black body. And while our focus on the fat Black body will be general in some places, we will talk specifically about the fat Black masc body—how it has been imposed on, forgotten, and dismissed within fat studies. This book doesn't exist anywhere else in the literary canon. There are many books on Black people, and there are many books on fat people, but there are so few that focus on fat Black people, and there are none that center on fat Black masc people's bodies. So that is what we will do here. We will add to the few works that have begun to bridge a necessary gap between Black studies, fat studies, and gender and sexuality studies.

In a sea of necessary memoirs and "how-to" books, it is my hope to provide the literary canon with a text that will explore topics often interrogated separately, but rarely ever interrogated together. What does it look like to talk about policing, police violence, and prisons with regard to how the fat Black masc body experiences them? What does it look like to talk about health not as something the Black fat body has been removed from but rather as something created precisely for fat Black people, or the Black fat, to never have access to? What does it look like to talk about Desire/ability as a form of systemic violence that, too, was designed as a building through which the Black fat could not enter? How has gender encaged the Black fat? How do wars on our body, like the War on Drugs and the War on Obesity, overlap and intermingle? What is the utility of "body positivity" if it only seeks to provide one with a false sense of confidence rather than to liberate all from that which cages the body? In this book, these are some of the questions we'll explore, and ultimately answer, together.

As a fat, Black, trans-nonbinary disabled person, I know the complexities that come with living in this body with these identities. I imagine that you do too, or you're looking to learn about those complexities. You opened this book because, at the very least, you acknowledge that anti-Blackness and anti-fatness have something to do with one another—even if that acknowledgment is only that you read the words on the cover of the book. And that is why I'm writing and ultimately why I care about this book. A curious mind can be the start to someone's understanding, and someone else feeling seen, heard, and understood. I value that.

When I started writing years ago, it was with the intent to ensure that our stories were documented well and that history tells those who come after me the full story. And that is why *you* should care about this book. Out there is a reality where fat Black folks are experiencing the harms of anti-Blackness as anti-fatness and need this book to give them the language to determine why it is harmful or give them a sense of comfort to know it is not happening to them in a vacuum and there is something they can do about it. Black liberation is the end goal, and for it to happen, fat liberation must also be part of that goal. Not "body positivity," but freedom from the confinements of cages—as Roxane Gay refers to the body—altogether.

In a post–body positive world—by which I mean a world subsequent to the formation of body positivity—at any given time on any given day, if someone fat posts a picture to social media or wears a bathing suit to the beach, they're met with one of two types of comments: comments intended to uplift or comments intended to cut deep. "You're so brave," someone might say. "I love this confidence" might be another one. Or perhaps, "I wish I had your confidence" or "Love the skin you're in!" find their way to the comment section. On the contrary, comments intended to do harm, like "You need to lose weight," "Stop glorifying obesity," or "This is disgusting," can also oftentimes be found under a fat person's pictures—especially when that person is Black. Generally, the harm in the hateful comments are understood as such, at least to most decent people. However, not many people understand the harm in the comments intended to be affirming. What could be so bad about complimenting someone's confidence? Or wishing you had their confidence? Or encouraging one to love all of who they are?

The issue with all of these comments is that, at their core, they suggest that self-love is enough to eradicate anti-fatness and that if you just accept yourself, or love who you are, that somehow the methodical violence of anti-fatness—housing, employment, etcetera—is no more. This is what is violent about "body positivity"; it is benevolent anti-fatness in that it is masqueraded as some sort of semblance of acceptance for fat people when it is, instead, an opportunity for Thinness to reroute, but not give up, its hold on fat people's collective liberation. As a politic, Thinness is a system that seeks to subjugate and ultimately eradicate fatness and fat people. Body positivity takes up this mantle through abandoning a fat politic—which ultimately insists on a world wherein fat people aren't discriminated against or marginalized for their fatness, and as such, people aren't categorized by the size of their bodies—and replacing it with one that makes a desire to lose weight a qualifier for the type of fat person that's worth celebrating and being nice to. And it is this type of fat person that is allowed to "love the skin they're in." Because the love they're being tasked with is conditional, by which I mean it is assumed that they want to lose weight and therefore will only have to temporarily love that skin. In other words, it passively demands that fat folks change their own bodies rather than explicitly demanding that the world in which we live shifts how it understands and responds to fat bodies. Which means that there is nothing necessarily positive about body positivity. "Bad fats," as they're affirmingly referred to in fat acceptance spaces, aren't *allowed* access to this movement because their end goal isn't to lose weight. This leaves "good fats" as the only fat people who "deserve" to love themselves and feel confident in their bodies. By "good fat" I am referring to the type of fat people whose acceptance of their body is contingent on their ability/desire to decouple their fatness from the prescribed actions fat people are supposed to take to be regarded as "healthy"—actions that are assumed will one day make them thin. "Good fats" are perhaps fine with not losing weight but must obsess over exercise and "healthy" eating to justify their fat body. And yet, whether one is a good fat or a bad one, these comments are always violent. Self-love, even a radical one, cannot and will not disrupt or bring an end to systemic violence.

In her book *The Body Is Not an Apology: The Power of Radical Self-Love*, Sonya Renee Taylor writes beautifully about radical self-love, describing it as an island on which self-confidence and self-esteem sometimes go to vacation, but do also vacate. At great length, she explores radical self-love in juxtaposition to self-acceptance, where she describes self-confidence and self-esteem as the "fickle cousins" and self-acceptance as the "scrappy kid sister" to radical self-love. Taylor asks the reader, essentially, to go back to their beginning. Beings we call humans were not born with hatred for their body or other people's bodies, and as such, she argues that this is integral for one to be able to embody or truly arrive at "radical self-love."

In sociological terms, what she is naming is that, through various social institutions, human beings are socialized—or taught—to hate their bodies and that there is a moment in our own lifetime where we did not look at ourselves through a lens of hate and disgust. These points are brilliant and fundamentally true. Where Taylor and I depart, however, is here: irrespective of how much internal work one does for themselves, the systems under which they live that actively lay claim to their bodies are not and cannot be reversed through any introspection or outward radical self-love. These socioeconomic political structures do not need the type of reform that a radical self-love would suggest, but rather they need total destruction. If we go back to the beginning, if we pull up the roots, unless the social institutions through which we were initially socialized are destroyed, we can only ever return back to the place we left. There is a particular connection between destruction and love. In this case, if we love ourselves and the people around us, we must also be committed to destroying the World in which we and they are actively harmed. This means that if love, of self or of others, is to play a role at all in any liberatory efforts, it must be a starting point and not an end. If self-love is where we start, it must be the driving force behind our continued struggle; otherwise, we become stagnant and immovable, fixated on always challenging how we see our bodies and never getting to the place where we no longer have to interrogate our bodies at all.

Radical self-love, as Taylor writes, is necessary cultural work. It challenges our relationship to our own bodies and to other people's bodies, and that will always be a work that can make our realities after the destruction of the World better than they were before, but it does not demand more than that because it cannot demand more. The Black fat does inherently exist as a metaphysical, political entity, but this does not inherently make one a revolutionary or a radical. If one plans to see the Beyond—a place in which we live without qualifiers, conditions, or labels meant to harm and subjugate our being—more work has to be done. Right now we live in a world of systems, all of which affect the body, some that are familiar in name, and some that are less so—systems of Desire/ability, health, the overall diet and medical industrial complexes, policing, prisons, and gender. There is tangible work one must do to destroy the ontological violence which engenders, or forges the path for, what is known as structural violence. Unless and until there is a reckoning with the conceptual, an evaluation of just how un/impractical this violence is, love of self will never be the answer to oppression nor will it ever be guaranteed. Because, while it is true that the violences of this World are happening *to* the body, the violence is not created *by* the Body.

The Body—an entity of sorts, or the flesh we are born into—is not what creates the violence. What creates the violence is an ideology and the power to enforce it, interpersonally or systemically. This means that whether or not you love on, show up for, and transform how you view *your* body, the structure of the World does not shift. This is, again, the harm of "body positivity." It cannot produce anything more than a quasi-self-confidence, and even that is conditional because it—for a long time now—has not been asked to. Body positivity individualizes something that is bigger than the individual.

At the beginning of this chapter, I wrote that this book is important because it can very well serve as the proof someone may need to know they are not experiencing the violence of anti-Blackness and/as anti-fatness in a vacuum; body positivity does not have that same commitment. For us to inch toward a tomorrow not limited by the confines of today, we have to interrogate the structures that actively marginalize our bodies and beings, and we have to destroy all that is attached to those structures. Neither body positivity nor self-love brings us to that pivotal point; the point beyond this World. By this, I mean that this World—one in which the Slave / the Other / the Black are produced—is the only World to have ever existed, at least ontologically/metaphysically. It is true that beings lived and breathed before this moment in time, but it is anti-Blackness, colonialism, and capitalism that form and shape the place we now refer to as the World. As such, the Beyond—the place we have not yet seen—is not and cannot be determined by what existed before now, but rather it will be created by acknowledging what about "the now" succeeded at making the World uninhabitable. In other words, this is the only world I will reference in this book because this is the only world in which the Slave / the Other / the Black exist, and that is the beginning of the World.

It's important that I restate this: In this book, you will read about the body. And not just any body, but the Black fat body. And while our focus on the fat Black body will be general in some places, we will talk specifically about the fat Black masc body—how it has been imposed on, forgotten, and dismissed within fat studies. That is my focus—the effects and affects of anti-fatness as anti-Blackness, and vice versa, and how that materializes through Desire/ability and Desire Capital, health by way of the medical and diet industries, policing and prisons, and gender, particularly as it relates to fat Black trans men, trans masculine folks, nonbinary people, and cisgender men.

The capitalization of varying words throughout this chapter and the entire book (Beautiful/beautiful, Ugly/ugly, Human, and Slave) is not only about what you *are*, but also what is assigned to you through the identities you hold. One reaps the structural and often interpersonal benefits of being Beautiful when they are white or have light skin, when they are cisgender, when they are thin, when they are non-disabled, and when they are not disfigured. One is Human—insofar as this particular category exists in opposition to Blackness—when they are white, and therefore, the Human is not the Slave / the Other / the Black. One's body is their own, but how Bodies are collectively engaged—and where they exist in proximity to power—is dependent completely on what identities one embodies.

Pretty Ugly:
The Politics of Desire

Janet Mock—celebrity writer, producer, director, and trans activist—wrote a beautiful essay in 2017 detailing the ways in which she experiences and benefits from "pretty privilege," even as a Black trans woman.[1] In the essay, Mock writes that as she started to be perceived as a girl, she was "let in." She saw that people started to stare and smile at her, she was offered seats on the bus, she was more heavily complimented on her appearance, and she was offered drinks at the club. This is, as she tells it, partly how she experienced "pretty privilege." In many ways, this essay created room for a widespread conversation on how prettiness contributes to how we experience the World.

However, Prettiness, with a capital P, is about much more than one's appearance, and it requires one to reckon with what it means to experience structural advantages over someone who is Ugly. When I capitalize the P in Pretty and the B in Beauty, or the U in Ugly, it is to name who does and does not have access to Desire Capital—that is to say who owns or embodies more or less of the identities that grant one access, power, and resources. More to the point, "pretty," "beauty," and "ugly"—all with lowercase letters—are subjective. They are not identities but are rather determined by the individual. Rooted still in anti-Blackness, but are not structural identities. Pretty, Beauty, and Ugly, however, are determined by the structures through which people are marginalized for their Blackness, their gender(lessness), and their bodies. Beauty standards, especially in the United States, are predicated on anti-Blackness, anti-fatness, anti-disfiguredness, cisheterosexism, and ableism.

As such, people who are Black, fat, disabled, and/or trans more generally do not have access to Beauty. However, as with all capital, one can embody identities that are valued in modern society and still also hold identities that are marginalized, which is why the term "privilege" is not quite specific enough and often does not go far enough. Desire is complex. Privilege insinuates that there is a possibility that you can opt out, and that if you don't *feel* pretty, then you can't possibly benefit from Prettiness or suffer the violences of Ugliness. Desire/ability politics and Desire Capital, however, suggest that one does not need to feel pretty to be Pretty; one does not need to feel beautiful to be Beautiful; one does not need to feel ugly to be Ugly. How one benefits or suffers from the subjugation of particular people is not determined by their feelings; it is determined by the identities they embody.

Desire/ability politics is the methodology through which the sovereignty of those deemed (conventionally) Attractive/Beautiful is determined. Put another way, the politics of Desire labels that which determines who gains and holds both social and structural power through the affairs of sensuality, often predicated on anti-Blackness, anti-fatness, (trans) misogynoir, cissexism, queer antagonism, and all other structural violence. It is intended to name the social, political, and economic capital one obtains / is given access to through their ability to *be* Desire. By this I mean that Desire is about much more than being desired; it is about one's ability to always already be positioned as the very embodiment of the thing(s) that make(s) one Desire/able.

For this reason, when talking about Desire, I employ language like Desire/ability politics, libidinal economy,[2] and Desire Capital. More directly, they each speak to the structure and metaphysics of Desire, Beauty, Prettiness, and Ugliness as things to be traded and saved as with any other economy. In this way, one can be insecure about how they appear, or not *feel* pretty, and still have access to Beauty, Desire, and Prettiness.

Insecurities are often taught as something to be afraid of, to be ashamed of, to run away from. People are taught that the way they feel about their bodies is their own moral failing and therefore their own responsibility to hold. We are all often socialized into believing that if we are insecure, then we are weak, incapable, or ugly and that all of those things are bad things to be. Many internalize that—especially those who exist furthest on the margins, like the Black fat.

But what if Insecurities are worth embracing, particularly for the Black fat? What if Insecurities are not a moral
failing of the individual, but rather an inadvertent critique
of a society that seeks to punish, harm, and abuse Ugly
people who dare to name that their perceived "flaws" are
only named as such because of anti-Blackness?

In many ways, and in other words, Insecurities are a
response to the violences Ugly people are forced to endure.
And so often, the people deemed Ugly are fat, Black, and
trans—people who are positioned outside the scope of Desire
and are thus faced with hypercriminalization and other violences against their Being.

"Insecure" is an adjective. It is a word intended to describe
or name a characteristic of a person, place, or thing—otherwise known as a noun. "Insecurity" is a noun. It is intended
to name a state of being, a response to a possibility of danger.
While "insecure" does the job of classifying one's (perceived
negative) feelings about their body and Being, "insecurity"
seeks to name the *response* to having no protection, the
response to being harmed. It lights the path to what leads
Ugly people to feeling unsafe, unconfident, and uncared for.

In *On the Politics of Ugliness*, Nina Athanassoglou-Kallmyer
gives a comprehensive summation of Ugliness as a politic,
wherein she lays out the history of the Ugly/Beautiful dichot-
omy in art history, literature, and aesthetic theory. In that
same collection, editors Ela Przybylo and Sara Rodrigues
write: "Ugliness or unsightliness is much more than a quality
or property of an individual's appearance—it has long func-
tioned as a social category that demarcates access to social,
cultural, and political spaces and capital" and that "our

aesthetic, political, economic, sexual, and social discomfort with ugliness" even affects and effects our relationship to and "dislike of ugly spaces, ugly buildings, dilapidation, and disrepair." In *Saving Face: Disfigurement and the Politics of Appearance*, Heather Laine Talley notes that "ugliness matters for us all, but it particularly matters for those with bodies deemed as ugly" and that "ugliness in itself becomes a way for barring a person's access to status, work, and love, functioning as an absence of capital."

"Persons" and "bodies" refer more specifically to people who are marginalized by race, class, (dis)ability(-ies), fatness, age, and gender. As such, Ugly is political. It is the determiner for who does and does not work, who does and does not receive love, who does and does not die, who does and does not eat, who is and is not housed.

The only logical step following the acceptance of Ugly as political is that Insecurity, too, must be political. If the politicization of Ugly leads to the social, political, economic, and physical death of a person, they are bound to feel unprotected, uncared for, and unconfident. To that point, Insecurities are valid. It is okay for us to be insecure in bodies that are constantly beat on and berated. Those Insecurities don't change the reality of what anti-fatness, or overall Ugliness, is and what it does. In fact, those Insecurities better contextualize it.

You can't beat people down forever and expect that they never feel the effects of that continued beating.

Insecurities are not a personal indictment; they are an indictment of the World. Being that this is the case, people deemed Ugly should run toward Insecurity. Not as a trauma to inform their politics—as it is dangerous to navigate the world of politics through trauma rather than an informed praxis—but as a political tool that aids in developing their understanding of and relationship to oppressive power structures.

The World is set up in this way: to be Ugly is to be a Monster; to be a Monster is to be the Slave; to be the Slave is to be the Other; to be the Other is to be unDesirable; to be unDesirable is to be the Beast. A metaphysical, ontological chain to pieces of flesh never intended to navigate this reality. And while Ugly people may not have control over that, what they do control is the ability to reclaim and redefine the meanings of these words. They can learn Ugliness and Insecurity more intimately as parts of who they are—particularly and especially under this imperialist white supremacist capitalist patriarchy.[3]

In a speech she gave in 2011 titled *"Moving Toward the Ugly: A Politic Beyond Desirability,"* Mia Mingus prefaced some important questions with a very important introduction:

> We all run from the ugly. And the farther we run from it, the more we stigmatize it and the more power we give beauty. Our communities are obsessed with being beautiful and gorgeous and hot. What would it mean if we were ugly? What would it mean if we didn't run from our own ugliness or each other's? How do we take the sting out of "ugly?" What would it mean to acknowledge our ugliness for all it has given us, how it has shaped our brilliance and taught us about how we never want to make anyone else feel? What would it take for us to be able to risk being ugly, in whatever that means

for us. What would happen if we stopped apologizing for our ugly, stopped being ashamed of it? What if we let go of being beautiful, stopped chasing "pretty," stopped sucking in and shrinking and spending enormous amounts of money and time on things that don't make us magnificent? Where is the Ugly in you? What is it trying to teach you?

The Ugly in all who are marginalized for their bodies, Blackness, and gender is trying to teach that Insecurity is important too. And so to add to her important questions, I would also ask: What would it mean if we were more insecure? What would it mean if we did not run from our insecurities or anyone else's? How do we take the sting out of "Insecurity"? What would it mean for us to acknowledge Insecurity for how it has informed our politic(s)? What would it mean for us to lean into Insecurity as a political tool in which we free ourselves from insisting that we perform "perfection" and total confidence in order to advocate for our collective liberation? What would happen if we stopped apologizing for our insecurities, stopped fearing them, stopped trying to shed ourselves of them?

Ugliness as political is what Frank B. Wilderson III is pointing to in his book *Red, White & Black: Cinema and the Structure of U.S. Antagonisms* when he uses Jared Sexton's words from a lecture to help define "libidinal economy." It is also what Sabrina Strings is describing in *Fearing the Black Body* where she writes:

Racial scientific rhetoric about slavery linked fatness to "greedy" Africans. And religious discourse suggested that overeating

> was ungodly . . . Not until the early nineteenth century in the
> United States, in the context of slavery, religious revivals, and
> the massive immigration of persons deemed "part-Africanoid,"
> did these notions come together under a coherent ideology.

As it relates to Desire/ability, fatness *as* Blackness—
which is to say that fatness is formed as a coherent ideology through the creation of (anti-)Blackness and therefore
does not intersect with Blackness, but exists with Blackness
itself—is what leads others to determining that fatness is
unDesirable. Similarly, it is those two things that keep thin
folks, and sometimes fat folks, from locating desire in the
Black fat. Said differently, it is this unDesire that creates the
margins that the Black fat is forced to live on. If the locale
of the subjugation of fat people is, too, at the genesis of
the objectification of Black subjects—and it is through the
unremarkability and unpleasantness of how fatness dressed
Black flesh that created the structures that necessitate the
marginalization of both identities[4]—then one can determine that Desire is at the root of the continued harm that
the Black fat navigates.

Statistics show us that fat people are less likely to be hired
for a job,[5] that fat people in America can legally be fired from
a job in forty-nine states for being fat,[6] that fat people are
more likely to be homeless,[7] that fat women are more likely
to be sexually assaulted,[8] and that fat people often die from
being misdiagnosed or undiagnosed.[9]

Make no mistake: fuckability as Desire/ability does not
mean that all bodies deemed fuckable are humanized, nor
does it mean that every person who has sex with the Black fat

sees them as living beings deserving of care. And it is often for this reason that fat subjects live with Insecurities. Being fuckable is determined by someone other than ourselves, and therefore it is completely about whether or not others locate desire in you. This desire does not have to come with an interrogated politic. It could very well be a fetish, predicated on the desire to only see fat people as sexual objects incapable of being more.

What fuckability as Desire/ability means is that Desire/ability is part of the Human experience, and being seen as unDesirable, specifically for the Black fat, is at the heart of what helps to maintain the separation between the nonHuman and the Human.

The hope, then, should not be to be Beautiful or Desirable. Instead, each of us should sit with why the idea of finding Ugly attractive is uncomfortable. Societally, there should be an interrogation of why Ugly people are asked to apologize for their Ugliness and to find ways to conform to Beauty rather than divesting completely from Beauty as a political concept. In that same vein, we should all sit with why we believe Insecurity as a concept must be a personal and moral failing rather than a result of systemic and social domination. I want us to know Insecurity as intimately as we know the marginalized pieces of ourselves: as valid, as identities, and as political.

This is an indictment of thin people—which includes people with gym bodies, people with athletic bodies, people who are slender, slim, or otherwise non-fat, as they all benefit from anti-fatness and cannot necessarily separate themselves from a politic of Thinness. This is an indictment of people who claim a liberatory politic but exist with a politic of Thinness. Thinness, as a politic, demands that one consume less, desire less, rather than make the demand that we end a World where what one desires would leave others without. On the surface, this means something as simple as the Black fat doesn't have to eat less. When interrogated more closely, however, this means that the Black fat doesn't deserve to have less access to housing; it means the Black fat doesn't deserve to have less access to employment; it means the Black fat doesn't deserve to have less access to proper medical care and to health care; it means the Black fat doesn't deserve to have less access to adequate clothing options. It means fat children don't deserve to be sent to fat camps—a project predicated on the idea that literal minors are undesirable and greedy. It means that fat women don't deserve to be believed less and assaulted more when sharing their stories of sexual violence—all of which is also predicated on the idea that fatness is unDesirable and they are thus unable to consent, because consent is reserved as an option only for those who are Desired.

This is to say that concepts like "greed(iness)" and "overconsumption" are the cages that breed Thinness. These concepts suggest that for one to be free, they must be thin—even if only in politic. Which is to say that one's disinterest in desiring fat Black people is harmful—not just for the fact that fat Black people deserve access to love but also because at the epicenter of our subjugation and objectification is unDesire. So to destroy anti-fatness and anti-Blackness, we must destroy Desire, Beauty, Thinness, and whiteness.

To state this more plainly: anyone who experiences sexual or romantic attraction, that also claims to be committed to fat people's liberation, who is uninterested in being in relationship with fat people (romantically, sexually, platonically, or otherwise) is, in fact, anti-fat. Wanting to alter your partner's body because it is "too fat" is anti-fat. Wanting to alter your own body because it is "too fat" or out of the desire to not ever *be* fat is fatphobic. Preferring to be with people who are not fat is anti-fat. And it is anti-fat because, statistically, thin people who hold these views are also the people in positions of power to deny the Black fat the materials and tools necessary for us to live.

Kiese Laymon wrestles with this a bit in his book *Heavy: An American Memoir,* specifically as it relates to sexual violence experienced by fat Black boys—a story so often untold.

In the beginning parts of *Heavy,* Laymon discusses how he felt that he was his sexiest self when Renata, one of his mother's students, put her breasts in his mouth, when she touched him, and when she breathed like she enjoyed what her body was feeling. He wrote about just how unsexy he would feel when she'd come over to his house and not touch him or let him touch her.

The story is further complicated when Laymon reveals that Renata was his babysitter and he had not yet reached the dawn of his teenage years when these acts of molestation began.

Laymon complicates our understandings of sex, sexual violence, and Desire by ushering us from a layered conversation around the hypersexualization of fat Black boys due to anti-fatness and Desire/ability politics, to an even more complex conversation about the fat body and what it is forced to endure for the sake of perceived pleasure and Desire/ability.

Several years ago, I penned an essay where I discussed a few of my encounters with sexual abuse, and my relation to Laymon is a result of the sexual abuse we both were forced to endure. Often, I don't feel sexy unless I'm pleasuring someone else's body through sex. In those moments, my body is most desired, and my body is not often appreciated outside of sexualized context.

When Laymon writes about his "thighs and calves" not being "muscly enough," I read an embarrassment that is not foreign to me. I empathize with how his lack of muscularity would sometimes keep Renata from touching him, and though she was sexually abusive, the feeling of being unwanted was nonetheless difficult to bear. Laymon's experience of abuse from Renata was further explored when he watched her have "fully naked" sex with her muscular boyfriend, highlighting again the extent to which sexual violence is psychologically disturbing and emotionally wrangling.

The feeling that your gut is figuratively and literally keeping you from experiencing what it's like to wrap your whole self around someone and for them to do the same to you is almost suffocating. As sad as it is, the feeling of your body being a physical barrier in sexual contact is oftentimes what we have to process before we can ever even consider that what we've experienced is sexual abuse.

I know what it's like to not process your assault for the deadly act that it is because fat people, generally—but fat Black boys and bois, specifically—are taught (sometimes, inadvertently) that we cannot be sexually assaulted, that we should appreciate when our bodies are being touched in any way, even when the behavior is violent.

Fat people are sexually assaulted, but the confines of gender limit whose stories are told. Overarchingly, fat people are not believed when they are victims and survivors, and yet, fat women courageously share their stories despite the risks. However, seldom do we hear from victims and survivors who are fat Black boys, and the lack of adequate and accessible data to support the claims of abuse does little for our supposed credibility. And it is for this reason that I write this from the personal. Because not only is the personal political, but the political has not made room for data beyond the personal.

Fat Black people forced into boyhood—whether we actively understood ourselves as such or not—are sexually abused all the time, and our invisibility as victims and survivors further demonstrates the ways anti-fatness is detrimental to the minds and bodies of fat Black boys/bois and must be eradicated in full.

I have known sexual assault more intimately than I have known most of my sexual partners, both when I was being forced into boyhood and now as a fat Black trans-nonbinary person. And part of what caused me to be slow in recognizing these encounters as assault/rape is the thought that I had to be grateful. For a long time, I had not processed those abuses because I was still working past the crossroad at which the hypersexualization of Black boys and the gaslighting of fat survivors meet. There is an exhaustive history of Black boys, bois, and men being fetishized and hypersexualized because of their dicks, their "hard" demeanor, and the animalistic characteristics assigned to their being and existence. This is exacerbated when the Black masc person is a fat one or is read otherwise as "large." While there is no clear evidence that Mandingo or warrior fights were real or used as forms of entertainment,[10] the very idea of such a reality is always already violent because it is formulated by the belief that Black cisgender men and other Black people to whom the illogics of "maleness" are assigned are necessarily expendable and their bodies are useful only as punching bags and modes of punishment. And as we will explore later in the book, it is this that so often leads to the murder of the Black fat.

There is also a long history of fat Black people, especially Black women, not being believed when they accuse men of rape. Many are even assaulted by police when they report. So for the Black fat, which lives with the heightened fear of being hypersexualized while simultaneously never being desired, this story rests heavy in our hearts.

To this point, sexual violence is not foreign to me. What is necessary for me to contend with, however, is just how much my body being read as that which belonged to a Black woman caused me to be assaulted by the type of men who engaged me.

The first time I can recall being violated by a man, I was around eight. At the time, I was perceived as a Black boy who had more ass and more thighs than boys were supposed to have. Black boys are supposed to be athletes. They're supposed to carry their weight proportionately or not at all. They are supposed to be thin, or at least a little muscular, and not really fat. Whatever their size, they were never supposed to look like the "little fast Black girl on the block." The one whose breasts formed a little earlier than expected. The one whose ass was just a little too round for men to resist. The one whose body moved differently when she walked. Though I was, in fact, an athlete, that body that people so easily read as "fast" was my own. I had the weighted thighs, the pants that didn't really fit, the ass that moved without being prompted to. And because I did, I quickly learned that my body was not my own.

bell hooks defines patriarchy as "a political-social system that insists that males are inherently dominating, superior to everything and everyone deemed weak, especially females, and endowed with the right to dominate and rule over the weak and to maintain that dominance through various forms of psychological terrorism and violence."[11] In *Mama's Baby, Papa's Maybe: An American Grammar Book*, Hortense Spillers writes of the "loss of gender" or an altered reading of gender for Black people—particularly and especially Black women—after slavery through the "ungendering" of their body.

This made evident to me that the violence my body has long endured was the ungendering of my Being, particularly due to the ways in which patriarchy shows up through anti-Blackness, anti-fatness, heterosexism, and misogynoir—a term coined and proliferated by Moya Bailey and Trudy. Black women, while mostly described as "strong" and thought to not be able to experience pain, are still oftentimes viewed as "vulnerable" and "weaker"—the latter most often being what informs the former. They are weak because they are strong; they are strong because they are weak. They are

assaulted because they are strong; they are weak, and therefore, they are assaulted. They are fast until they are slow; too
slow until they're fast. They are girls until they are women;
they're always women, even when they are girls. Cisgender
men, and the way they rationalize these violences against so
many bodies, are walking contradictions.

It is this that forces me to grapple more deeply with
my assaults. The type of men who engaged my body, who
I understand as down-low (DL) and straight-assumed, still
held intimate relationships with women, or led others to
believe so. My body—full and weighted—waited for no one
to touch it, and yet it was touched anyway. Over. And over.
And over. And over again. It was engaged in such a way, in
part, due to the fact that this body is and has always been
removed from gender. For these men, my body provided a
comfortability usually found only in "fast" girls void of any
and all perceived vulnerability. Said again, my body was wel-
coming—even well into my adult years—because, frankly, it
made these men feel that they were fucking a woman without engaging the power dynamic therein. And this is not to
say that men who are DL are into boys, nor is it to excuse the
violence of trespassing against someone else's body, but it is
to say that the only need for a DL identity is to protect the
masculinity of those not directly assumed to be queer while
harming those of us for whom queerness is inescapable.

To provide a point of clarity: this is not intended to com-
pare my experience to that of little Black girls robbed of
their girlhood and Black women robbed of their womanhood, but rather this is to name the severity of the violences
transgressed against them and the overall harm of applying

gender to flesh always already being ungendered or experiencing "racialized disgendering," as Milo W. Obourn names it in her book *Disabled Futures: A Framework for Radical Inclusion*:

> Disgender is neither an assimilation to dominant gender identities, nor a complete rejection of or removal from dominant narratives of gender, but rather a way of thinking about the complex and disabling (in both the sense of limiting access and in the sense of providing a social identity and epistemically valuable way of being in the world) ways that gender intersects with our other social identities.[12]

If these assaults fell so confidently on my body, one that was thought to have belonged to a boy, one can only imagine the aggregated harm many Black girls and women have been forced to endure. Patriarchy acts as a system that assigns power to cisgender men, or men assumed to be cisgender, and employs hegemonic masculinity at the expense of people directly harmed by gender(ed) violence. By this, I mean that men, especially those who are cisgender and heterosexual, while also negatively affected by this system, are empowered to hold dominance over women and all other people impacted by gender(ed) violence. This is, to my understanding, where the harm forged onto and around my body, bodies like Laymon's, and other bodies like ours interact most with misogynoir and ungendering.

Sydney Lewis writes in "I Came to Femme through Fat and Black" that she "came to Femme as defiance through a big booty that declined to be tucked under, bountiful breasts that refused to hide . . . Through shedding shame instead of shedding pounds," and this forced me to consider how the fat Black fem(me) body is perceived, especially in the Black South. Fem(me) bodies like Lewis's—ones with breasts and booties that would be described with adjectives like "voluptuous" and "busty"—have often defied standards of beauty, of womanhood, of femme-ness and femininity, so much so that, for as far back as the enslavement of African people, fat Black women in the South have long had a history of being assigned the role of caregiver/nurturer. They act as the Mammy.

The Mammy caricature, dating back to 1810, originated as an image to advertise the mythological unification of the South. Enslaved fat Black women were assigned the duty to care for white children. Their bodies, oftentimes used and abused, were thought of as a symbol of loyalty, unity, and care. Writer and historian Jesse Parkhurst writes that "[the Mammy] was considered self-respecting, independent, loyal, forward, gentle, captious, affectionate, true, strong, just, warm-hearted, compassionate-hearted, fearless, popular, brave, good, pious, quick-witted, capable, thrifty, proud, regal, courageous, superior, skillful, tender, queenly, dignified, neat, quick, tender, competent, possessed with a temper, trustworthy, faithful, patient, tyrannical, sensible, discreet, efficient, careful, harsh, devoted, truthful, neither apish nor servile."[13] And though all these descriptors were used as a way to market the Black women caring for white children—thus, creating a "unified South"—what is never made public is the sexual abuse her body endured; the fact that she, too, was still nothing more than property; that she was just an image who was still denied the realities of resources, freedom, and a true role in society.

This is a truth, an imagery, that is still central to the Black South. The feminization of the Black fat body is salient in our culture. We deify the imagery of our grandmothers cooking, cleaning, and caring for us with their low-hanging arm fat. We reminisce on the moments we shared out on grandmama's/mama's/auntie's porch, looking out into the field, where she imparted all of her knowledge and wisdom into us. And still, as Lewis writes, these women are deviant in that their bodies refuse to take up a different form. Ingrained in the DNA of the (Black) South is the belief that fatness, especially when it rests on a Black woman, belongs to non-fat people; that the only acceptable time to love/touch/assign femininity to a fat, dark-skinned Black person's body is when it is performing for someone else, and especially when that body belongs to a woman. This sense of entitlement is what leads to the sexual violence against "little fast Black girls" who had shapely and fat bodies. To that same point, this is what feminizes the body of little fat Black boys and bois who own a body most often associated with Black women or completely removed from gender entirely.

My assaults, though made possible by heterosexism and anti-fatness, too, have all happened in conversation with misogynoir and the way in which men engage bodies that "belong" to Black women—even when those bodies actually belong to Black girls, Black boys, and Black adults who are not women.

As bell hooks says in *Understanding Patriarchy*, boys are propagandized into the order and stipulations of patriarchy by teaching them to feel pain but to never express it. This, I believe, is something that men know, even if they cannot name it. This is the cause for this sort of intracommunal (both Black and non-heterosexual) violence: these particular men intend to explore their sexuality with bodies that don't make them too uncomfortable, with the expectation that they'll never speak of it again; that they'll internalize it and move on with their lives; that they, fat boys, own bodies that are meant for women, thus designed to violate, but will/ must adhere to the patriarchal teachings that they should never be courageous enough to speak of the trauma afflicted by those who have trespassed against them. That is why my assailants felt comfortable with engaging with me normally whenever they would see me outside of those moments of assault, and I imagine that this is also part of the reason why Renata used Laymon's body as an outlet. The idea is that if boys are to be boys that will one day be men, they'd have to accept their part in patriarchy.

As previously stated, the Black fat is misdiagnosed by medical professionals, are skipped over for jobs and housing, sit at the crux of harm committed by dieting and diet culture, experience heightened interactions with police, leading to state-sanctioned brutality, and are showcased as the evil that waits in children's stories and beastly gluttons in religious texts. In various ways, the world has normalized the teachings that fat Black people are not Desirable and, thus, fat and Black bodies are deserving of the abuse they endure.

Anti-fatness is coercive in that it teaches people to believe that the bodies of fat Black folks are only supposed to endure pain, never pleasure; that their very existence is always defined by Death, never Life; that their value, if any is assigned at all, is wrapped up in their ability to perform. They have to be the Mammy archetype or, for the fat, dark-skin Black masc person, they must exist between what I refer to as the Fat Albert and Mark Henry tropes—purposed with the sole role of caring for everyone other than themselves or positioned as animalistic and consistently tough. Now that I understand myself as a person not restrained by the confines of gender, I have found myself detangling the web of patriarchy in my life and being more committed than ever to being sure that those "little fast Black girls" never have to experience the worst parts of patriarchy again. That is what we must all be committed to. We must commit to the complete eradication of the Mammy caricature. We must commit to the total deconstruction of the patriarchy.

What I am really naming here is the complicatedness of feeling both affirmed and harmed by your assault because your body is never really your own when you're fat and Black, and the trauma you arrive at upon realizing that there is no affirmation in touch intended to harm—or at least unintended to be sure of your consent.

The solution doesn't have to be a complicated one, however. For those who are raising fat Black boys or children otherwise read as masc(uline), be sure to share with them how beautiful they are, always. Teach them that weight loss is not a requirement for them to be beautiful, even if they will never know Beauty. That their body is not an extension of their beauty but is, instead, central to their beauty. That they can be as sexual as they want, but their bodies don't have to endure being hypersexualized by anyone. That abuse of their bodies—through medicine, sex, religion, and other social institutions—is not something you tolerate.

It is necessary that fat Black kids are taught that Insecurity exists in direct response to Beauty and Desire. This sets the foundation for how they will engage their bodies and the bodies of others around them. They should know that Ugliness is structural violence just as intimately as they know that anti-Blackness is. To use Insecurity as a political tool means to war against a desire to conform to Beauty, and in doing so, it means waging a war against the idea of health, Thinness, and the foundation on which anti-Blackness and anti-fatness thrive.

There must be a commitment to destroying a World wherein one is abused and subjected to structural violence for having bodies too large and too dark for care.

Health and the Black Fat

According to the World Health Organization, health is the state of complete physical, mental, and social well-being and not just the absence of disease or infirmity.[1] As I interpret it, this means that for one to be healthy, they must not only be non-disabled but must also be in an environment that allows for them to feel mentally secure, psychically safe, and socially well. As such, this means that Black people—especially those of us who exist with multiple marginalized identities—are always already unhealthy because we are always already unsafe. The creation of race through slavery was precisely intended to make Africans, with their blackened or "stained" skin, subjects. They became objects to be subjugated, poked and prodded, and turned—at least through language and especially through the ways in which they were engaged—into Beasts. Said differently, built into the very fabric of modern society, of the World—created by Europeans and sustained by anti-Blackness—is the idea that the Black, which is to name the Slave, is but an object and a subject, and therefore has no need for, or right to, safety or wellness. The Slave was and has always been removed from wellness and safety, both through the total subjugation/ domination and objectification of their Being.

In fact, for "race" to be constructed, the Slave had to exist—and had to exist as the antithesis of health—so that European physicians, anthropologists, and other eugenicists could determine what set the Slave apart from, as J. F. Blumenbach called them, the Caucasian; that being the "degeneration," or the corruption, of the Slave's body from the Caucasian.[2] For all intents and purposes, Blumenbach created race, and did so as to differentiate the Human from the Slave. These scientists based the idea of health on what Africans could and could not withstand and created health "issues" based on what Africans *would not* withstand. Take, for example, Samuel A. Cartwright. In 1851, Cartwright named two "illnesses" that were exclusively found in Africans. The first of the two was what he called "drapetomania," which was a mental illness that caused the Slave to run away. The second one was called "dysaesthesia aethiopica," which was a sort of weakness or lack of work ethic that Africans would develop if they were not enslaved or otherwise in the possession of white enslavers. His suggested treatment for both illnesses was to wash their open wounds, drape their bodies in oil, beat them with a leather strap, and force them to work in the field—specifically when the sun was beaming.

These "illnesses" were specifically about characterizing the Black who dared to believe they were deserving of health, whereby they were deserving of safety and wellness. Cartwright deemed them "psychologically abnormal and inept,"[3] and this would essentially birth what we now understand to be "scientific racism." Medical apartheid, as named by Harriet Washington, is foundational to the creation of race—which is the creation of the Black, which is the creation of the Slave. For as long as there is a Black, there is a subject to be experimented on; for as long as there is a subject to be experimented on, health will always already be inaccessible to the Slave. And as this is the case, health is a framework in which no Black person can ever fit. This is especially true for fat Black people.

The Belly—or fatness—is yet another reason for why the Beast—or the Black—can and will never have access to health. In *Fearing the Black Body: The Racial Origins of Fat Phobia*, Sabrina Strings masterfully details how fatness on the Black subject's body set the precedent for how fatness would be engaged in the United States and the world as a whole. Fatness was once seen as something to aspire to, something that was attractive. The reason for this, however, was because, at the time, fatness signified sociopolitical and economic power. What Strings makes clear in *Fearing the Black Body* is that it was fatness's alignment with whiteness that really made it attractive to Europeans. When Europeans saw Africans for the first time and saw that their bodies looked like them but their skin did not, it was then that antifatness was established as a coherent ideology. Because fatness had become blackened (and Blackened), it could only ever be impure and beastly. As the Slave represented capital and forced labor, fatness could no longer be about status and power, so it became about greed and ungodliness.

Strings argues that the fear of fatness and the preference for thinness are, principally and historically, not about health but rather they are ways to legitimize race, sex, and class hierarchies. I agree that anti-fatness is not about health insofar as the systemic bias against fat people is not predicated on a desire to see Black people mentally secure, psychically safe, and socially well. However, because that is true, I would also argue that anti-fatness *is* about health to some extent. For anti-Blackness and anti-fatness to be legitimate subjugating and objectifying structures, their existence had to be predicated on a Thing unobtainable by Black fat subjects. That Thing is health. In other words, to legitimize race, sex, and class statuses, health had a job to do. That job was to ensure that the Black—which is, too, the fat—was always fixed to be something that Black fat subjects could not be. This leads to the birth of the medical industrial complex—an institution built and sustained by race scientists and eugenicists dedicated to the continued Death of Black fat subjects. Said again: to be Black and fat is to always live as Dead, and "health" ensures that. As opposed to one's literal and physical state of being dead, Death signifies that one—particularly, the Black fat—walks as Dead, talks as Dead, lives and breathes through Death, and that one is ontologically always already socially Dead. In this way, so-called race scientists and eugenicists used, and do still use, the Black fat as capital, that is, products on which they build anti-Black and anti-fat structures like "health" and the medical industrial complex with the intent to maintain a hierarchy—a social World order.

Strings states that race works to repress "savage blackness" while also disciplining whiteness. I believe that fatness and health do something similar. Fatness and health, like race, are also double agents. They are all used to tell Black fat people who and what they are, but they are also used to tell white people who they should not want to become. When they fail to model that, it can be deadly for them too. Not in the same way as it is for the Black, but deadly as a result of even unintentionally aligning oneself with what exists as the obverse of whiteness.

Health, in name and in action, has always existed to abuse, to dominate, and to subjugate. The medical industry, the health care industry, and the diet industry all exist to maintain a culture intended to "discipline" those whose bodies refuse to—and, for many, simply cannot—conform to the standards of health. Modern society enforces exercise as a punishment for this very reason. We are not taught to exercise for the sake of enjoyment, nor are we taught to enjoy our bodies in motion. We are taught, per contra, that we exercise so that we can be healthy, and that health must look opposite of fat. This means that health is punishment. So much so that there are entire camps dedicated to forcing children to exercise for the sake of weight loss. We call them fat/boot camps. The entertainment industry has created an entire market built on shaming adults into weight loss through reality television. We call it *My 600-lb Life*, *The Biggest Loser*, and *1,000-lb Sisters*. These industries lead to real psychological harm, physical pain, and death.

In 1999, a fourteen-year-old girl by the name of Gina Score died because of forced exercise and a lack of care around fat children's bodies. Gina, who had been part of a camp run and operated by military veterans, had been tasked with a 2.7-mile run. In the middle of that run, Gina fell on the ground and began gasping for air. Soon after, she began foaming at the mouth and hallucinating. After four hours of her instructors laughing at her—while drinking soda, no less—and accusing Gina of faking, a doctor came outside and called for an ambulance immediately. Gina's organs had failed. She had died.[4]

In an extreme case like this, many would call what happened to Gina abuse. In fact, many did. Gina's case went on to introduce a national conversation around the mistreatment of youth in boot camps, and erected new laws and policies in juvenile correctional facilities. But not only was Gina abused, she was murdered. She was murdered because her instructors found no value in her fat life. The abuse did not start and end with Gina's collapse or with the instructors' negligence, though; the abuse began with the idea that Gina ever needed to be punished for her weight in the first place. It could be argued that Gina was not originally at the camp for her fatness but was instead there to "correct" her "bad" behavior, but so much of the behavior being read as "bad" is structured by her fatness. At the nucleus of her punishment was a push for weight loss as discipline, and health and wellness as ways to correct or "fix" bad or broken behavior. It is also what led to her death. She was neglected, at least in part, because she was fat. The nearly three-mile run she was forced to do, the idea that she was faking what would be her own death to avoid exercise, the fact that her instructors left her to lie in the sun while they drank sodas—a beverage people have long shamed fat people for drinking—were all a targeted response to her fatness. And it killed her. She was murdered by a culture designed to punish fat people at the behest of "health" itself.

Children are sent to these boot camp–like weight loss programs to be shamed for their weight, manipulated into believing that the abuse they're forced to endure is about being accepted instead of being punished for owning a body that looks different from what the rest of the world sees as normal. Fat kids are being penalized for their bodies, "whipped into shape," disciplined for something the rest of the world views as an offense and a breach of an imagined moral code.

Everyday life for fat kids is like a fat camp. Even for those who have never been to one. Mistreated for having bodies that take up more room than humans are allotted. Harmed for showing up in a world where Thinness is the universal norm. This is a very targeted form of abuse. There is no other way to put it. Forcing exercise and diets, especially onto children, is an attempt to punish them for their fatness and that *is* abuse.

The blame rests on the medical industrial complex, which thrives off harming fat people. It rests on the diet industrial complex, which seeks to steal from fat people. And most yet, the blame rests on the collective and societal commitment to making exercise and fitness about weight loss and punishment rather than feeling good in one's body and in motion. Through this commitment, whole industries have been developed with the intent to warp the minds of fat people—and people attempting to avoid becoming fat. We know them best as weight loss programs.

In September 2018, Weight Watchers published a press release that revealed the company's new name, new tagline, and its overall "new" focus.[5] The focus, according to the release, was "no longer weight loss" but rather "all around health and wellness." The reality, however, is that a rebrand in name only does not shift the material reality that WW, as they are now known, is just another result of a two-hundred-plus-year phenomena: diet culture and the diet industrial complex—which I define as the written and unwritten pact between food, medical, and health care industries and billionaires with a vested interest in building and sustaining a socioeconomic system under which fat people are stolen from and harmed through dieting.

The diet industrial complex—and multibillion-dollar weight loss industries like WW—is a project that thrives only on the (societal) commitment to the subjugation of the Black, and moreover, the Black as the fat. Dieting, or yo-yo dieting as it's more accurately referred to, is but a temporary food plan with only temporary solutions to something that is not inherently a problem. By this, I mean that diet culture was never intended to successfully produce results for anyone who invested in these programs, and the overall commitment to weight loss is inherently anti-fat. On diet culture, Virgie Tovar once wrote:

> Diet culture does one thing very successfully: it alienates us from our natural relationship to food and movement, things

that we as human beings have had a relationship to since the beginning of time, and which we cannot live without, and it sells them back to us as "diet" and "exercise" with the promise that with hard work and self-denial we can achieve a state worthy of love, respect, and admiration.[6]

But neither diet culture nor diets are needed to do this. Of people who diet, 95 to 97 percent tend to "fail."[7] Not because they aren't committed, not because they are following them incorrectly, but because dieting demands that you do whatever it takes to shed pounds—even if what it takes requires you to harm yourself—instead of encouraging one to do what makes them feel good in their body. Especially if whatever that is does not require them to lose weight. Because the capital is in teaching people to hate their bodies; it's in how much we value thinner bodies and how much guilt we associate with foods we enjoy.

Diet culture creates language like "guilty pleasure" and "cheat day," which teaches one to associate foods that they love, that make them feel good, and that they actually find enjoyable, with harm. And while it is taught that diets are necessary for one's survival, many of these short-term diets can lead to high blood pressure, heart disease, diabetes, and more. In fact, one study found that men with a fluctuating weight were at an 80 percent higher risk of dying than men who were "overweight."[8] Another study found that women who were yo-yo dieters were about 82 percent less likely to reach and maintain their ideal weight.[9]

Revisiting Tovar's quote, what one can find at the core of diet culture are two very specific forms of structural violence that already plague our society: patriarchy and purity culture.

As mentioned earlier in the book, bell hooks defines patriarchy as "a political-social system that insists that males are inherently dominating, superior to everything and everyone deemed weak, especially females, and endowed with the right to dominate and rule over the weak and to maintain that dominance through various forms of psychological terrorism and violence."[10] Purity culture emphasizes the evangelical Christian teachings that girls are supposed to be abstinent until marriage and that queer people are supposed to be "freed from all sexual immorality."

These two things matter in the conversation of diet culture because at the crux of this industrial complex is the idea that dieting is for the weak to become strong—associating weakness with femininity, hence diets being marketed mostly to women, and strength with muscularity and masculinity—and for fat people to deny our appetite. In a literal sense, it *is* psychological terrorism. From its origins, diet culture was intended to force fat people to deny their desires, and the concept was introduced by Sylvester Graham, who insisted sex was immoral and food could control morality.[11] In this way, diet culture and the diet industrial complex is a prison—the same prison that keeps people caged in the proverbial "closet" and locked behind the bars of purity.

In "Flaunting Fat: Sex with the Lights On," Jenny Lee talks about "the closet" as it relates to fat queer people's bodies. It is important not only to this conversation, but for abolitionists altogether. In the essay, Lee talks about how fat people are often forced into a "closet" through diet culture,

specifically, in the same way that people who are deemed—
or self-identify as—sexually deviant often are. Diet culture
imprisons fat bodies, by which I mean that diet culture is the
closet; it confines them to a cell—one that is inescapable—
with the intention to keep fatness hidden/unseen/behind
bars. As Strings stated, it is not about health but rather the
repulsiveness assigned to fatness by others. For this reason,
fat liberation is an abolitionist affair, abolition is a queer
affair, queerness is a fat affair. Liberation for each of them
is linked.

What can be added to this, though, is just as the closet
is a room that many feminine gay men and butch lesbian
women can rarely take rest in for safety, it is also a room that
many fat people cannot fit in. What this means is that the
closet is always already deadly and antagonistic, whether
you are in it or outside of it. No one can sit comfortably
inside of diet culture. It is the prison. It is the closet. It's fixed
and designed, specifically, to be uncomfortable. Its sole purpose is to incarcerate, to make sure that no fat person has the
freedom to just be—whether they are dieting or not. In this
way, the closet is not a place of refuge. It endangers many
people by keeping them bound and doesn't offer safety to
people who exist too far outside of the borders of the identities it's projected to keep safe. If you are "too fat," or "too
gay"—and, really, "too Black"—the closet can't offer safety.
But irrespective of whether one is in or outside the closet,
what is always being demanded of the Black fat and the
Black queer, in particular, is that they commit themselves
to repressing or doing away with their queerness and their
fatness. The promised safety can only be found in Thinness

and heteronormativity, which is to say, safety is only offered to white people through whiteness.

A company like WW capitalizing off the fear and hate-mongering of the "Obesity Epidemic"—which does not exist—is anti-fat and capitalistic. Billions of dollars are spent on these weight loss programs to maintain diet culture, but the majority of Americans are fat. Not only does this mean that intentional weight loss is a scam, but it also means that diet culture is a scam—especially when considering that more and more studies are finding that weight loss does not improve health biomarkers.

Anyone who still has a vested interest in diet culture, intentional weight loss, and/or these types of programs is making the active decision to invest in systemic anti-fatness, anti-Blackness, ableism, misogyny/-noir, and capitalism.

Weight loss does not have to be something worth celebrating. Said differently, "lost" weight is celebrated because modern society teaches that the weightiness of fat peoples' bodies is inherently burdensome, cross-bearing, backbreaking, onerous. Not on fat people, but on the people who surround them. Therefore, there's no regard for whether a person is well when they "lose" weight because the societal desire is to not have to be concerned with the Ugliness of fatness—by which this means the Ugliness of the Black. How the fat is misplaced or "lost" does not matter, just as long as it is gone.

However, fatness—both as an identity and as the literal tissue—has value. Which means that the celebration of "lost" weight is much more of a celebration of thievery. It is the theft of a fat person's ability to see themselves as someone who matters, theft of a person's right to see their body as neutral rather than inherently bad, a breach of consent on how a person enters into a relationship with their fat body. It is a war on the body, particularly and especially for the Black, and it is one that has been introduced and reintroduced since the Transatlantic Slave Trade.

Black, Fat, and Policed

Eric Garner, Mike Brown, Tamir Rice, Walter Scott, Samuel DuBose, Alton Sterling, George Floyd. These are just a few of the people who made headlines, national news coverage, and whose hashtagged names took over social media timelines after they were each murdered between 2014 and 2020.

On July 17, 2014, Eric Garner stood on the streets of Staten Island, as he so often did, selling untaxed cigarettes. It was the second time that month he'd been approached by police, and it would have been his third arrest that year.[1] Onlookers recorded the encounter that would soon be seen by millions. As he lay on the ground, surrounded by a swarm of New York police, Eric Garner was placed in an illegal chokehold by Daniel Pantaleo. Garner offered eleven pleas for breath with the words "I can't breathe." Pantaleo never let up. Soon after, coverage on Garner's murder began to home in on his body. The US representative for New York's second congressional district, Pete King, urged a grand jury to not indict Pantaleo because, as he tells it, the police were only doing their job to take down a "350-pound person who was resisting arrest."[2] According to King, Eric Garner's cause of death was not the illegal chokehold but rather his asthma, his heart condition, and his "obesity."

During a disciplinary trial, which did not happen until five years after the murder of Eric Garner, the medical examiner who conducted Garner's autopsy—Dr. Floriana Persechino—claimed that while she did find that the chokehold "set off a lethal sequence of events," that "even a bear hug" could have killed him due to his "fragile health."[3] Pantaleo's attorney, Stuart London, homed in on Garner's health too. During his cross-examination, he pointed to a report from NYPD's doctor, Eli Kleinman—who had not personally examined Garner—wherein he stated that Garner was "predisposed to morbidity and mortality" and that his death was brought on by a "heated argument followed by a physical struggle."[4]

The disciplinary hearing was supposed to answer one question: Did Pantaleo use an illegal chokehold? Instead, it centered on whether Garner could withstand or could have avoided experiencing an illegal chokehold ... or a bear hug.

It is true; Eric Garner was a six-foot-two, 395-pound man with asthma, diabetes, and a heart condition.[5] However, before his interaction with Pantaleo and the other police officers that swarmed around him, what he was *not* was dead. This means that, no matter how much of an untamable

Beast he was made out to be by the lawyers over the case, the grand jury, the medical examiner and other doctors, and the media, what led him to his dying breath was a police officer's arm around his neck.[6]

As Black communities around the United States mourned the death of Eric Garner, Mike Brown was murdered.

On August 9, 2014, Mike Brown's name became an international hashtag in a matter of minutes. The world watched as his body lay flat in the streets of Ferguson with no medical care, forced to soak in his own blood for four hours before being hauled away. Weeks after murdering Brown, Darren Wilson gave his account of what transpired that day. In his testimony, Wilson described Brown as "aggressive" and "eager to fight."[7] To illustrate how powerful Brown was, Wilson described him as "Hulk Hogan," and claimed that as he shot Brown, he "bulked up to run through the shots."[8] He called Brown "crazy"; he called him a "demon"; he claimed that Brown was "looking through him" and that he made Wilson feel like a "5-year-old" in comparison.[9] At the time of the shooting, Darren Wilson was six feet, four inches tall and 210 pounds. Mike Brown was six feet, five inches tall and 290 pounds.[10]

Wilson made himself the perfect victim. Though he and Brown were built similarly, and only one of them had a weapon in their possession, Wilson knew that for him to evade any consequences, the only "weapons" Brown needed to possess were his fatness and his Blackness. What Wilson described was not another human being. He described a Beast, a Monster, something otherworldly. From that moment forward, we witnessed countless murders of Black men and masculine people, and what most of these people had in common—alongside Blackness—was fatness or an otherwise larger body.

Three months went by, and as Ferguson protestors were still rallying in the streets, there was another life lost. Tamir Rice.

On November 22, 2014, Tamir Rice was playing in a park in his neighborhood in Cleveland. He was spotted by a neighbor who called the police to report "a guy pointing a gun at people"[11] in the park. On this call, the neighbor also warned that the "guy" was "probably a juvenile" and that the gun was "probably fake."[12] As police arrived, in under two seconds, Timothy Loehmann jumped out of his car and shot at Rice twice—hitting him once—from four feet away. Following the shooting, Detective James Mackey asked the FBI agent who had arrived on the scene if he'd assumed, as he walked up to aid Rice, that the boy was older. The agent responded, claiming he assumed Rice was "at least 18," and explained that Rice was "big" and was "the size of a full-grown man." From the moment he died, the blame for his murder was the size of his body—not the officer who shot him.

Investigators also claimed that they thought Rice was much older because of his size. This was a claim they were so deeply committed to that they conducted interviews specifically to search for photos of Rice holding a gun or photos where Rice appeared to be older compared with the photos being shown on the news. Three months after the shooting, the investigators conducted a follow-up interview with the neighbor who called the police. In that interview, he claimed that Rice looked to be "around 20-years-old"[13]—a much different claim than the initial one he made saying that Rice was probably a juvenile. As with Garner and Brown, the police officers and investigators were attempting to write Rice as the Beast in their story. Their intent was to make him the monster that had to be killed; a tale as old as time about the hero who kills the villain for "the greater good." At twelve years old, Rice stood at five feet, seven inches and weighed two hundred pounds. He was indeed larger than the average twelve-year-old—a fact that only matters if one believes police have a right to murder Black people, or that police should exist at all. Nevertheless, prosecutors Tim McGinty and Matthew Meyer leaned into that fact. They also argued that Rice was "big for his age" and "could have easily passed for someone much older."

Just over four months later, Walter Scott was gunned down.

Scott's story, and the others that follow—barring George Floyd's—are very important to include here, not only because of how high profile they were but also to showcase that anti-fatness and the inherent anti-Blackness within these cases is not always something that is explicit. Walter Scott, Samuel DuBose, and Alton Sterling were never specifically engaged like Garner, Brown, Rice, or Floyd, and yet their stories matter in this context, too, because anti-fatness is always already a factor in determining who/what lives and who/what must always die.

On April 4, 2015, Walter Scott was stopped by ex-officer Michael Slager for a broken taillight as he pulled into the parking lot of an Advance Auto Parts store in Charleston,

South Carolina. Slager approached Scott's vehicle, and when he returned to his car, Scott bolted from his vehicle into a vacant lot. Slager followed him on foot and shot his taser at him. Once they were both in the lot, they had a physical altercation where Slager shot his taser at Scott once more. Scott was able to escape, and as he started to run away again, Slager shot at him eight times. Five of those rounds hit Scott in the back, killing him almost instantly. In the initial report, Slager claimed that he feared for his life because Scott took his taser during their altercation. To solidify this claim, Slager staged the scene.[14] As Scott lay in his own blood, Slager grabbed the taser he alleged Scott took away from him and placed it near Scott's body to make his story appear true. That story would later be proven untrue with the release of a video that showed not only the shooting but Slager planting evidence as well.

Just three months later, there was another shooting: Samuel DuBose.

On July 19, 2015, Samuel DuBose was pulled over by Ray Tensing—former officer of the University of Cincinnati Police—for a missing front license plate. When DuBose could not produce his driver's license, Tensing demanded that he remove his seatbelt as Tensing attempted to open DuBose's front door. In protest, DuBose yelled "I didn't even do nothing" and held his door shut while turning the key in the ignition. Tensing yelled at him to stop, and in a matter of seconds, grabbed his firearm and set off one round into DuBose's car—killing him instantly. As Tensing told the story, he fired his weapon only after DuBose started to drag him with his car. His body camera, however, showed that the car was not in motion before he fired his gun. The county prosecutor claimed that the shooting was "asinine," and that Tensing "lost his temper" because DuBose "wouldn't get out of his car quick enough."[15]

Perhaps that's true, but the larger issue is not just that DuBose would not get out of his car quick enough, but that someone who looked like DuBose—a Black man who was larger in size—would disobey the demand of someone who was higher in stature, even though Tensing was far outside his jurisdiction as a campus police officer. The shooting was a result of Tensing's inability to control/tame/properly capture this Beast.

Just over a year later, Alton Sterling was murdered.

On July 5, 2016, Alton Sterling was shot and killed in Baton Rouge by two police officers who were called to apprehend "a man in a red shirt" standing in front of a convenience store with a gun, selling CDs. Officers Blane Salamoni and Howie Lake II were filmed pinning Sterling down, with one of them straddling his legs as the other kneeled down beside him. In the captured footage, Sterling is visible from the chest up and from his lower legs. His right arm lay by his side, his left arm not visible. In a matter of moments, one of the officers yells, "he's got a gun" as they begin to open fire on Sterling.[16] While being interviewed, witness to the murder, Abdullah Muflahi, stated that Sterling was shot six times. Muflahi claimed that Sterling never once went for a gun in the midst of this altercation with police. He continued by saying that Sterling's gun was, in fact, "never visible at any point." According to the police, Sterling warned that he had a gun, which Salamoni took as a threat. The officer yelled "gun" and shot Sterling three times. According to Muflahi, the two officers yelled again for him to "get on the ground"—despite him already being on the ground and having already been shot—before firing three more rounds into Sterling. He died on the scene.

Two years after the shooting,[17] the Baton Rouge Police Department released the footage they had from the officers' body cameras showing what happened before the shooting. In that footage, the officers became physical with Sterling almost immediately upon their arrival. They attempted to arrest Sterling, shot him with a stun gun, and, after he got back up from that, they tackled him to the ground. They never saw a gun. All they saw was Sterling, his CDs, and a Beast they could not tame. Sterling lay on his back as the officer wrestled with him. As with Garner, Sterling's greatest weapon was being the Black and the fat—always already animalistic and dangerous in nature.

Nearly four years after Sterling's murder, the world witnessed the murder of George Floyd.

On May 25, 2020, George Floyd was apprehended by Minneapolis police after being reported for allegedly using a counterfeit $20 bill. Seven minutes after the report was made, police arrived on scene and approached the vehicle Floyd was sitting in with two others. Former officer Thomas Lane pulled out his gun and demanded Floyd get out of the car. Lane grabbed Floyd to pull him out of the car, and from there it is alleged that Floyd resisted being handcuffed. Once handcuffed, however, he became compliant. Minutes later, several other officers arrived on the scene, including the officer who would soon murder Floyd, Derek Chauvin.

Chauvin pulled Floyd from the passenger side of the police car, forcing him to the ground. Though already handcuffed and lying on his stomach, face planted into the ground, officers began to further restrain Floyd. Chauvin placed his knee firmly into Floyd's neck, and Floyd released the plea "I can't breathe" more than twenty times. For nine minutes and twenty-nine seconds, Chauvin kept his knee on Floyd's neck and told Floyd to "stop talking" because it takes "a heck of a lot of oxygen to talk." Floyd exclaims, "Can't believe this, man. Mom, love you. Love you. Tell my kids I love them. I'm dead."[18] Six minutes into the nine-minute-twenty-nine-second time period, Floyd reportedly "flailed" for about a minute due to seizures until he fell silent.[19] Bystanders yelled for them to check his pulse. One officer did and said that he "could not find one." No other officer moved, and Chauvin's knee remained on Floyd's neck for almost four more minutes before Floyd was given any medical attention.

In a matter of thirty minutes, Floyd went from buying a pack of cigarettes at a local convenience shop to lying unconscious in the street after being restrained by police. While Floyd was not fat, he was a larger man, and how his life and body were treated—both in that moment and following— was largely a result of that.

Floyd was six feet, four inches tall and 223 pounds and lived with several health issues, including hypertensive heart disease and coronary artery disease, according to his autopsy.[20] Floyd's family's lawyer rightfully denounced the official autopsy upon its release after noting that it ruled out asphyxia—or being strangled—as a cause of death. In that autopsy, medical examiners claimed that Floyd had drugs in his system, concluding that it was "potential intoxicants," along with his underlying medical conditions and the restraint by police, that led to his death. The Floyd family commissioned a second autopsy and that one concluded that he died of asphyxiation due to neck and back compression.

As has already been seen, police, lawyers, and medical examiners will use the size and medical conditions of a Black person murdered by police as a reason for why their murder was their own fault. But Floyd did not die because of his heart condition or any other illness he had;[21] Floyd was murdered by an anti-Black officer who was committed to taming Floyd's body in whatever way he felt necessary. That was his goal. He wanted to show off the dominance and power he had over Floyd, as every other officer examined here so far has done.

These stories are not often told in full. Many times, the narrative around the murders of Black people by police is centered only on their Blackness. However, it is essential that the inherent fatness read onto Black subjects, and the health often always disassociated from the Black fat, is part of that narrative, too. As already covered, the Black is the fat; the Belly is attached to the Beast. This means that police and policing, especially in the United States, exist *because* the Black fat is to always be caged, just as a Beast is always to be captured.

In her book *Becoming Human: Matter and Meaning in an Antiblack World*, Zakiyyah Iman Jackson adds to an argument presented by Saidiya Hartman in *Scenes of Subjection: Terror, Slavery, and Self-Making in Nineteenth-Century America* that "the process of making the slave relied on the abjection and criminalization of the enslaved's humanity rather than merely on the denial of it." She continues by saying that "humanization is not an antidote to slavery's violence; rather, slavery is a technology for producing a *kind* of human." By this, Jackson is arguing that the subjectivity of black(ened) flesh is what constitutes, or establishes, what she calls "the human" and "the animal"; that, since there is a "liberal" or "Eurocentric humanism," the Black and the animal—or, as I call it, the Beast—coexist as one. As such, being Human is not the answer to anti-Black violence, but rather for anti-Black violence to exist—for there to be a Slave—there must be the Human. The Black as the Beast, and the Beast as the Black, are essential to the maintenance of "the Human"—even and especially as the Black/Slave/Abjected are removed from Humanness. In this way, Black subjects are not denied humanity, or dehumanized through slavery, but rather are forced to become the Beast of humanity; the lowest on the scale of hegemonic humanity and placed among "the animal."

Jackson adds to this, first for her book and later adapted for an essay titled "Animality and Blackness":

> As long as "the animal" remains an intrinsic but abject feature of "the human," black freedom will remain elusive and black lives in peril, as "the animal" and "the black" are not only interdependent representations but also entangled concepts. While there are particular Euroanthropocentric discourses about specific animals, just as there are particular forms of antiblack racialization based on ethnicity, gender, sexuality, and national origin, for instance, these

particularizing discourses are in relation to the organizing abstraction of "the animal" as "the black." To disaggregate "humanity" from the production of "black humanity," the one imposed on black(ened) people, assumes one could neutralize blackness and maintain the human's coherence. But the neutralization of blackness requires the dissolution of discourses on "the animal" and vice versa, but that is, to say the least, unlikely because "the animal" is a mode of being for which Man is at war. What is more plausible is that attempts to neutralize blackness and "the animal" will continue to be in practice, if not word, a means of discipline and eradication.

As the Black is the Beast, the Black fat is always already criminalized and engaged as something, and some Thing, that needs to be neutralized, euthanized, put down.

Slavery was already an institutionalized entity in the United States by the time the first slave patrol was developed, which meant that the Black—more directly, the Black fat, the Slave—was already claimed. In America, policing can be traced back to a few different sociopolitical moments in history, the most prominent of them being slavery. North Carolina, known then as the Province of Carolina, was home to America's first slave patrol in 1704, which would be considered the first police department in the South. This is made clear by K. B. Turner, David Giacopassi, and Margaret Vandiver in "Ignoring the Past: Coverage of Slavery and Slave Patrols in Criminal Justice Texts" where they state:

A legally sanctioned law enforcement system existed in America before the Civil War for the express purpose of

> controlling the slave population and protecting the interests of slave owners. The similarities between the slave patrols and modern American policing are too salient to dismiss or ignore. Hence, the slave patrol should be considered a forerunner of modern American law enforcement.

The idea behind a police force, and overall policing, was that since the Slave was property, and property had socioeconomic value, there was a need for an institution that could help maintain order (among the enslaved) should they ever become disruptive (to the institution designed to cage them). This meant that the slave patrol had three duties: to catch all enslaved people who ran away from the plantation, to take any and all action they deemed necessary to terrorize the enslaved as to prevent any type of revolt, and, to borrow from the words of Foucault, part of the duty for the slave patrol was to "discipline and punish" any enslaved person who disobeyed the order and control of their enslaver(s). After the Civil War, the role of the slave patrol was modified and taken over by groups who saw a need to continue in the tradition of capturing, abusing, and ultimately murdering the Black—most notably, the Ku Klux Klan (KKK). But by this time, institutionalized police forces were already developed in almost every major city in the United States, and many of those officers took it upon themselves to use their position and power to work alongside the militia members who had not yet become part of the American policing institution. Following the Ku Klux Klan Act in 1871—a law that disallowed state officials who were engaged with the KKK from tramping on the alleged rights of Black people—that all changed. More institutional police forces were established across the South, and this birthed what we know now as the "Jim Crow era." The sole job of the police, irrespective of how often the name changed, was to participate in a system forged to capture and put down the Nigger, which is the Black, which has always, too, been the fat.

What this means is that the Black—which, as noted, is always already the fat—was the first "criminal" insofar as the categories "Black" and "fat" were created specifically to be criminalized, subjugated, and objectified. If the Black fat was always already designed to be criminal, unlawful, outlawed, then the Black fat can only ever exist on the run, as a fugitive because there is never a "home," the Walking Dead among the living. To borrow words from Cheryl Harris,[22] whiteness *as* property means that humanity—and the rights, privileges, and freedom reserved for those who possess it—is denied to the Black fat always already. To this point, as has been covered in the previous chapter, for the Black to exist so too must the fat. If we agree that this is the case, then what also makes the Black "criminal" is the fat(ness) assigned to the Black. Policing is not just an institution; it is a social agreement, an assignment for those who have a(n) (in)vested interest in the control of the Black fat. For policing to have existed as an institution there must have first been a social need, by which I mean desire, voiced by thin, wealthy white people for the Black fat to be policed. As such, "criminality" is not easily dismissed by the so-called dismantling of groups like the KKK, nor is it abolished alongside the abolition of police forces. Total abolition, then, must mean the destruction of the World through which the Black fat is always made the Beast, the Other, the fugitive.

In the late 1990s and early 2000s—following the Clinton administration, which helped to cement the rapidly growing mass incarceration rates in Black communities—prosecutors in Cook County, Illinois, played a "game." This game's name was masked under the pseudonym "The Two-Ton Contest," but among the prosecutors and judges alike, the game was more affectionately referred to as "Niggers by the Pound." The sole objective was to be the first person to prosecute as many Black people, most of whom were men, it took to amount to four thousand pounds. The more one person weighed, the more points they were worth. Nicole Gonzalez Van Cleve, who is a professor in the sociology department at Brown University, inserts more details about this in her book, *Crook County: Racism and Injustice in America's Largest Criminal Court*:

> Here is how you play: Look at the weight of the defendant in the case file. Convict the defendant, and then tally the weight as a conquest to earn yourself points for pounds. One strategic tip: Convictions of the heaviest defendants are worth big points in the game, so you must offer them good plea deals, regardless of their crime, to incentivize the conviction of the fattest defendants. Be the first prosecutor to convict four thousand pounds of niggers and you win!

She continued, "Defendants potentially 'deserving' of longer sentences received short ones. Conversely, other defendants received harsher sentences not on the basis of their crime or the evidence against them, but according to their weight."

Police officers, with the help of policies implemented by presidents Ronald Reagan, George H. W. Bush, and Bill Clinton, fabricated evidence they knew would make it easier to arrest and convict Black people in Chicago. They forced people to assume the role of a witness to a crime so that they could give a false testament in court. They harassed and coerced defendants into making confessions of crimes they didn't commit—reminiscent of the infamous Central Park Five. And while officers did this, prosecutors awaited their opportunity to play courtroom games as judges sat idly by—even worse, turning their heads from the very obvious destructive actions taking place in their courtrooms, and even worse than that, joining in on the laugh before helping the prosecutors win this game. This was what followed the reform of slavery and the institutionalizing of police(ing).

Black feminist scholar and abolitionist organizer Angela Y. Davis further clarifies this in her book *Are Prisons Obsolete?,* wherein she provides the reader with a necessary comparative analysis on slavery and the prison industrial complex and on just how much the prison has been reformed and how many lives it still lays claim to despite that fact. She writes:

> Imprisonment itself was new neither to the United States nor to the world, but until the creation of this new institution called the penitentiary, it served as a prelude to the punishment. People who were to be subjected to some form of corporal punishment were detained in prison until the execution of the

punishment. With the penitentiary, incarceration became the punishment itself. As is indicated in the designation "penitentiary," imprisonment was regarded as rehabilitative and the penitentiary prison was devised to provide convicts with the conditions for reflecting on their crimes and, through penitence, for reshaping their habits and even their souls.

She continues, writing, "the penitentiary was generally viewed as a progressive reform, linked to the larger campaign for the rights of citizens."

In the third chapter she states, "It is ironic that the prison itself was a product of concerted efforts by reformers to create a better system of punishment. If the words 'prison reform' so easily slip from our lips, it is because 'prison' and 'reform' have been inextricably linked since the beginning of the use of imprisonments as the main means of punishing those who violate social norms."

The Black fat is constantly experiencing the harms of these reforms, even those camouflaged as abolitionist, because reform should never be a goal and we must go further than abolition as an end goal. The end goal must be a complete destruction of Society itself. The deaths of Eric Garner, Mike Brown, Tamir Rice, Walter Scott, Samuel DuBose, Alton Sterling, and George Floyd all relay this truth. For Scott, DuBose, and Sterling, their actual weight and health were not nearly as central to their stories as the others, but their bodies and size most certainly still mattered in how they were engaged and ultimately murdered. They, along with the others mentioned throughout this chapter, embodied exactly what the Slave, the Black, the Black fat have always been, which is to say that in an anti-Black, capitalistic World, they can only ever be the Other and that makes them Beasts.

Eric Garner, in an attempt to survive a World always already unsurvivable for people like him, was literally choked to death. Over untaxed cigarettes, he was engaged as an immediate threat even to the people who held enough sociopolitical power over him to kill him without immediate arrest. That was an intentional act of anti-fat, anti-Black violence—even if it is never named as such by the people who murdered him. There is a belief that fat Black people—in these cases, men—are supposed to withstand alarming amounts of pain, so much so that they can even survive being choked. Or, as an alternative, that whether or not they can survive the pain doesn't matter so long as they suffer it. This is why the officer didn't care that Garner couldn't breathe. The words "I can't breathe" didn't register as a warning because, to the officer, they were only proof of life. While "I can't breathe" became a rallying cry for Black people around the country, it became a slogan that officers around the country mocked with great pride—as if they were celebrating their best and latest kill, as though the officers' intent was to antagonize the animals that roamed the streets angrily before they made their next kill.

Mike Brown and Tamir Rice were both depicted and literally described as massive men—not boys. Despite being just eighteen years old and twelve years old respectively, their boyhood was killed alongside them in cold blood. Media and society alike compared Brown to an ape and a gorilla while the officer by whom he was murdered likened him to Hulk Hogan and described him with the ability to run through bullets.[23] It didn't matter that Brown had just graduated from high school. It didn't matter that Rice was only in the sixth grade. What mattered was that before the officers that murdered them both stood two giants, massive and uncontrollable animals, beings for whom "innocence" and childhood were never an afforded luxury. Anti-fatness as anti-Blackness, the Bellies of the Beasts.

Their murders were intentional. A study published by the *Journal of Personality and Social Psychology* in 2014 titled "The Essence of Innocence: Consequences of Dehumanizing Black Children" sought to determine how much Black children were treated differently from white children based entirely on their race. This study found that "black boys can be seen as responsible for their actions at an age when white boys still benefit from the assumption that children are essentially innocent." This study tested over 170 police officers—most of whom were white—in predominantly Black areas. The study, in which officers were tasked with pairing Black and white children to either large cats, like lions, or to apes, found that most of the officers paired Black children with apes. Those same officers, according to this study, were also more likely to use excessive force against a Black child in custody. Use of force was described as "takedown or wrist lock; kicking or punching; striking with a blunt object; using a police dog, restraints or hobbling; or using tear gas, electric shock or killing."

Walter Scott was running away when he was murdered, and in many ways this is reminiscent of the birth of policing. Scott's murder came as the result of a Black fat seeking safety—something that, much like with health, is inaccessible to the Black fat. As with enslaved people from literal plantations who sought freedom by fleeing the fields, or many "criminals" and refugees who cross borders seeking asylum, Scott ran *away from* what he recognized as danger in search of an imagined safety. Policing has a legacy, and that legacy is about much more than the continued criminalization, apprehension, and murder of the Black fat—its legacy is the formation of a World in which one is always the criminal, always the Slave, always the Black fat, and is therefore always running away from danger even as and because safety's locale is always unreachable.

This is all true, too, for Samuel DuBose, Alton Sterling, and George Floyd. Anti-Blackness, specifically as it relates to police brutality, cannot be divorced from anti-fatness. As such, the Belly cannot be separated from the Beast—which is to say that there is no Beast without the Belly, and there is no Belly without the Beast. Fat Black people—specifically men—experience police brutality at disproportionate rates because their "largeness" coupled with their Blackness is read as dangerous, destructive, and inherently violent.

It is for this reason that many of the men that crossed television screens and made national headlines after being murdered by police were both fat and Black. The years 2014 through 2020 made clear the inherent violence of policing for many. What those years and the many cases and hashtags that came along with them should also make very clear is that this type of violence works to silo the Black fat and is therefore only made possible through the Black fat's continued subjugation. Mike Brown, Alton Sterling, Walter Scott,

Eric Garner, George Floyd, Samuel DuBose, Tamir Rice, and so many others are testaments to this fact.

The focus on Black cisgender men here is not intended to suggest that it's them, and them only, who are in danger of experiencing the weight of police violence. Black cisgender women, Black trans women, and other Black trans people are also directly and indirectly harmed by police violence because of the ways that anti-Blackness and gender work together to create the conditions that endanger them. This is, instead, intended to provide a point of clarity for why so many, if not most, of the people who crossed television screens as victims of police murder were both Black and fat.

This war on fat people and Black people didn't start with slavery and jump immediately to the Black Lives Matter era. In many ways, wars waged on Black communities and fat communities between the 1980s and the early 2000s, through the War on Drugs and the subsequent War on Obesity, bound these structures together in ways that must be interrogated more intently.

5

The War on Drugs and the War on Obesity

I n March 2004, during a news conference with widespread coverage, the Centers for Disease Control and Prevention (CDC) published a report that claimed that obesity was "killing 400,000 Americans a year," and that it was becoming America's "number one preventable death"—surpassing tobacco. The CDC defines obesity as "weight that is higher than what is considered as a healthy weight for a given height."[1] Body mass index (BMI) is used as a "screening tool" to determine who is and is not obese. The report was published in the *Journal of the American Medical Association (JAMA)* which, at least at the time, was the most prestigious medical journal in the nation. Since Julie Gerberding, director of the CDC at the time, and other top

CDC scientists co-authored this report, it had the credibility it needed for waves of reporters and news outlets to publish it. It would soon lead to egregious and violent headlines across the nation about fat people, fat bodies, and the alarming rate at which they were allegedly dying from obesity. It would also be cited repeatedly by officials including then-Secretary of Health and Human Services Tommy Thompson, several members of Congress, and creators of weight loss drugs seeking to draw attention and funding to anti-obesity efforts. From that moment forward, throughout the rest of that year, public officials and other media platforms used that report as evidence that obesity was the greatest threat facing the American people, and as justification for what would eventually become a forceful and strapping diet industrial complex. This was the start of the "Obesity Epidemic."

There were a few public indictments of the *JAMA* report, starting with *Science* magazine in May 2004. In a report of their own, they wrote: "Some researchers, including a few at the CDC, dismiss this prediction, saying the underlying data are weak. They argue that the paper's compatibility with a new anti-obesity theme in government public health pronouncements—rather than sound analysis—propelled it into print."[2] This became, at least on record, the first acknowledgment of an emerging anti-fat theme within government, health, and science institutions. Soon after *Science* magazine's report, the *Wall Street Journal* published a story of their own that covered the errors in the study published in *JAMA*. On November 23, 2004, they opened their story with "America's obesity epidemic may not be as deadly as the government has claimed." Continuing, they wrote that the study "inflated the impact of obesity on the annual death toll by tens of thousands due to statistical errors."[3] On April 30, just a month after the later-disputed report was published, Dr. Terry Pechacek, who was the associate director for science in the CDC's Office on Smoking and Health, wrote in an email to his colleagues that he was "worried that the scientific credibility of the CDC likely could be damaged by the manner in which this paper and valid, credible, and repeated scientific questions about its methodology have been handled." After stating that he had warned two of the report's authors along with another senior scientist, Pechacek wrote, "I would never clear this paper if I had been given the opportunity to provide a formal review."[4]

According to J. Eric Oliver in his book *Fat Politics: The Real Story behind America's Obesity Epidemic,* Dr. Pechacek was right to worry. A more intentional look at the method the CDC used to produce these calculations indicated that the numbers were far from accurate. In his book, Oliver says:

> The CDC researchers did not calculate the 400,000 deaths by checking to see if the weight of each person was a factor in his or her [or their] death. Rather, they estimated a figure by comparing the death rates of thin and heavy people using data that were nearly thirty years old. Although heavier people tend to die more frequently than people in mid-range weights, it is by no means clear that their weight is the cause of their higher death rates. It is far more likely that their weight is simply a proxy for other, more important factors such as their diet, exercise, or family medical history. The

> researchers, however, simply assumed that obesity was the
> primary cause of death, even though there was no clear sci-
> entific rationale for this supposition.

In other words, the CDC contrived this number from an estimation after reviewing data that was thirty years old. It was never a calculated number concluded from their own intense research; it was a scientific guess made with the hope to punish fat people for their bodies. And it worked. The damage had already been done. The people and institutions who would stand to benefit from that report had already won, and it was the start of the modern genocide of fatness and fat people. As Oliver states, fat people do tend to die at higher rates than their thin counterparts, but it isn't because of their weight. Fat people tend to die at higher rates than thin people because doctors misdiagnose them, or refuse to treat them, due to their fatness.[5]

In January 2005, the CDC admitted that their 400,000 deaths number was a result of a "mathematical error,"[6] and in February of that same year—just after the CDC published a summation of the internal investigation that was launched following the initial report's release—the *Los Angeles Times* published a response to the investigation. Their report opened with this firm statement: "A controversial government study that may have sharply overstated America's death toll from obesity was inappropriately released as a result of miscommunication, bureaucratic snafus and acquiescence from dissenting scientists."[7] This would become the second public acknowledgment of governmental disarray that was leading the nation in one of the most violent pseudoepidemics in the nation's history.

In April 2005, just a year after the initial report was published, the CDC released another report—also through *JAMA*—wherein they not only offered a much smaller number of deaths per year due to obesity, but also claimed that "moderately overweight people" live longer than people at a "normal weight." The new report in *JAMA* cut the death toll to 112,000,[8] which was well under half of what was initially reported, but the damage had already been done. Around the world, people were using the CDC's original numbers as fuel for the war waged on fat people. The government allocated more money to scientists for research on the "harmful effects" of obesity; the number of plastic surgeries, particularly abdominoplasty—best known as a tummy tuck—and liposuction doubled in number from the start of the decade to the end of it; gyms became anecdotally known as "clubs of the 2000s," as gym memberships skyrocketed that decade; major diet industry companies, like Jenny Craig and Weight Watchers, changed their marketing schemes, which resulted in them raking in millions of more dollars for the diet industry.

The diet industry, at the time, was already well over a century old. Americans had been dieting and trying to lose weight for decades. But with this war waged on obesity, the early to mid-2000s are a pivotal moment in history for the creation of this modern diet industrial complex. The CDC's report cemented a growing belief: fat people were dying rapidly and the only solution was to kill them quicker—either through forcing them to transform their bodies or to die trying. Despite how theatrical that reads, that is what was being demanded of fat people. The goal was, and continues to be, to eradicate fatness. To do that, one was to either over-invest in dieting—which has proven to be ineffective—or die trying to reach an ideal weight defined by organizations like the CDC and WHO, either on an operating table or in a gym.

What is happening to fat people, the societal and systemic bias and marginalization they have to navigate, is in large part due to the one CDC report heard around the world. And to this day, the CDC continues to be at the fore-front of selling "obesity" as an epidemic.

But this was not the first time in America's history that a genocide would be declared on an entire community at the behest of this country's leadership. Just three decades before the start of the War on Obesity there was the genesis of the War on Drugs.

In the 1960s, drugs were a prominent part of the socio-political climate of the times. They became associated with juvenile uprisings, and in many ways, they became emblematic of the political and ideological contestation over harmful policies and practices by the United States government—arguments led mostly by Black and other marginalized people. As such, the government ceased all research on the safety of these drugs and, in 1971, former president Richard Nixon declared a war on drugs.[9] Nixon substantially increased the amount and power of federal drug control agencies in the country and bulldozed mandatory sentencing and no-knock warrants into the forefront of the legislation being passed at that time. Though it passed during his tenure as president, the legislation picked up momentum under Reagan's presidency in the 1980s. By the early 1980s, local police had used over 1,500 no-knock warrants, according to Peter Kraska, a professor with the School of Justice Studies at Eastern Kentucky University.[10] By the year 2000, that number had increased to 40,000 per year. In 2010, it increased to 70,000 per year. Of these searches, over 40 percent impacted, and continue to impact, Black homes[11]—including the home of Breonna Taylor who was killed in Louisville, Kentucky, in 2020.

Soon after that legislation was passed, Nixon placed marijuana in the most restrictive category of drugs, schedule one, where it would stay until it was reviewed by a commission led by then-Governor Raymond Shafer—a commission appointed by Nixon. Despite the concordant recommendation from the commission in 1972 to decriminalize the possession and distribution of marijuana—for personal use—Nixon ignored the report and did not adhere to the proposed recommendation.[12] Irrespective of this, eleven states around the country decriminalized marijuana possession between the years 1973 and 1977—a year in which former president Jimmy Carter ran and was elected on a platform inclusive of the decriminalization of marijuana. And in that same year, the Senate Judiciary Committee motioned to decriminalize the possession of up to an ounce of marijuana for personal use. But soon after, these efforts were left behind as former president Ronald Reagan ushered in what would become known as "mass incarceration" through his expansion of Nixon's war on drugs. The incarceration of people charged with nonviolent drug offenses grew from 50,000 in Reagan's first year in office to 400,000 by the end of 1997.[13] Stress levels and concerns induced by the fearmongering of the Reagan administration were high,

forcing upon mostly Black communities a proliferation of
arrests. By the end of 1999, over half a million Black people
were held in state or federal prisons. In 1980, the overall
federal prison population was 24,000. By 1996, the number
had grown to 106,000—the majority of which were arrested
for drug offenses. According to Kenneth B. Nunn in "Race,
Crime and the Pool of Surplus Criminality: Or Why the
'War on Drugs' Was a 'War on Blacks,'" from 1979 to 1989,
the percentage of Black people arrested on drug charges
doubled from 22 percent to 42 percent of the overall number
of drug-related arrests. Also during that time, the amount
of Black arrests for drug use violations grew exponentially
from 112,748 to 452,574—an increase of over 300 percent.

First Lady Nancy Reagan began campaigning against
the use, possession, and distribution of drugs, most notably
crack—a form of cocaine that can be smoked—and coined
the now infamous slogan "Just Say No." What followed was
disastrous and still wreaks havoc in Black communities
throughout the country. Ronald Reagan introduced zero-
tolerance policies in the mid-80s and Los Angeles Police
Chief Daryl Gates—who according to the Drug Policy Alliance once stated that "casual drug users should be taken
out and shot"—founded the Drug Abuse Resistance Education (D.A.R.E) program that would soon be implemented
in schools across the country despite there being no evidence stating that it was useful. This also meant, however,
that there was no widespread evidence that it was ineffective—an unsurprising failing of the United States' medical industry. The Drug Policy Alliance also states that "the
increasingly harsh drug policies also blocked the expansion

of syringe access programs and other harm reduction policies to reduce the rapid spread of HIV/AIDS,"[14] making the
War on Drugs not only a war on recreational use of drugs
but also on medicinal use. They continue:

> In the late 1980s, a political hysteria about drugs led to the
> passage of draconian penalties in Congress and state legis-
> latures that rapidly increased the prison population. In 1985,
> the proportion of Americans polled who saw drug abuse as
> the nation's "number one problem" was just 2–6 percent.
> The figure grew through the remainder of the 1980s until, in
> September 1989, it reached a remarkable 64 percent—one
> of the most intense fixations by the American public on any
> issue in polling history. Within less than a year, however, the
> figure plummeted to less than 10 percent, as the media lost
> interest. The draconian policies enacted during the hysteria
> remained, however, and continued to result in escalating
> levels of arrests and incarceration.

In 1994, John Ehrlichman—domestic affairs advisor and
top aide to Nixon, as well as a Watergate co-conspirator—
told investigative reporter Dan Baum a truth that had long
been understood but never really confirmed: the War on
Drugs was a legal way to criminalize and abuse Black people.
In his report, published in *Harper's Magazine,* Baum records
Ehrlichman saying:

> The Nixon campaign in 1968, and the Nixon White House after
> that, had two enemies: the antiwar left and black people.
> You understand what I'm saying? We knew we couldn't make

> it illegal to be either against the war or black, but by get-
> ting the public to associate the hippies with marijuana and
> blacks with heroin, and then criminalizing both heavily, we
> could disrupt those communities. We could arrest their lead-
> ers, raid their homes, break up their meetings, and vilify them
> night after night on the evening news. Did we know we were
> lying about the drugs? Of course we did.

In a recording of a conversation between Nixon and
Reagan, released by the National Archives in 2019,[15] Reagan—
who was the governor of California at the time—was quoted
saying, "Last night, I tell you, to watch that thing on television as I did . . . To see those—those monkeys from those
African countries—damn them, they're still uncomfortable
wearing shoes." At best, this was a conversation between two
anti-Black white men ranting about their hatred of Black
people. At worst, this was a collusion of two anti-Black white
men—both of whom held social, economic, and political
power—who met with the intent to forge a plan that would
help them leverage that power over the people and communities for whom they held a lot of hate. It was a success. The
war—that was and has been more accurately called a genocide, waged first by Nixon—has been continued by every
president that followed him, across party lines.

Following Reagan, Bill Clinton took office. Though he
initially campaigned on "treatment over incarceration," he
adopted the drug war policies of his Republican predeces-
sors and further expanded mass incarceration through the
implementation of like the 1994 Crime Bill—which included
a "Three Strikes" provision. That bill, which was opposed by

members of the Congressional Black Caucus, was proposed, co-authored, and signed by current Democratic heavy hitters like Joe Biden and Bernie Sanders. Like with Nixon and Reagan, Clinton helped to target and abuse working-class Black communities through continuing this so-called War on Drugs.

At the core of the War on Drugs is the Black, and at the core of the War on Obesity—even if not as explicitly so—is the Black fat. Black people make up roughly 13 percent of the American population, but about 51 percent of America's fat population. Obesity is determined by body mass index (BMI), something people have been taught is a direct measure of one's health. Over two hundred years ago, a Belgian man named Adolphe Quetelet created what we now know as the BMI. Quetelet was not a physician, nor did he study medicine in any capacity; Quetelet was a mathematician and a sociologist, and it was that on which the BMI was created. Quetelet is known for his envisioning of *l'homme moyen*—an image of what he understood to be "the average man"—which he developed through "the measurement of human features with the deviation plotted around the mean."[16] He began the development with the use of physical features of the human, who—at least as his work suggests—he understood to be cisgender white men. Those features included the chests of Scottish Highland regiment soldiers. After, he moved on to moral and intellectual qualities like suicide, crime, and madness. On Quetelet, Erna Kubergovic writes in the Eugenics Archive:

> For Quetelet, the average body presented an ideal beauty; the normal, conceived of average, emerged as an ideal type

to be desired. It was Quetelet that formulated the BMI, initially through the measurement of typical weights among French and Scottish conscripts. Instead of labelling the peak of the bell-curve as merely normal, he labelled it "ideal," with those deviating either "overweight" or "underweight" instead of heavier than average or lighter than average. Thus, while informed by statistics, Quetelet was still working within the medical context of the normal; that is, he envisioned the normal (i.e., typical) as the ideal or something desirable.

What he had created was the standard for male beauty and health, built only with white Europeans in mind and determined by something that measured whole populations and not individuals. By the twentieth century, Quetelet's work was being used as the basis of, and justification for, eugenics. And though all of his work in that time period was based in anti-Black race science, he was clear that the intent of the BMI was to measure populations to develop statistics. Aubrey Gordon, creator of "Your Fat Friend" and author of *What We Don't Talk about When We Talk about Fat*, wrote more on this in an online essay:[17]

By 1985, the National Institutes of Health had revised their definition of "obesity" to be tied to individual patients' BMIs. And with that, this perennially imperfect measurement was enshrined in U.S. public policy. In 1998, the National Institutes of Health once again changed their definitions of "overweight" and "obese," substantially lowering the threshold to be medically considered fat. CNN wrote that "Millions of Americans became 'fat' Wednesday—even if they didn't gain a pound"—as the federal government adopted a controversial method for determining who is considered overweight.

It was that second change, Gordon notes, that gave way to "a new public health panic: the 'Obesity Epidemic.'" Gordon continues:

By the turn of the millennium, the BMI's simple arithmetic had become a de rigueur part of doctor visits. Charts depicting startling spikes in Americans' overall fatness took us by storm, all the while failing to acknowledge the changes in definition that, in large part, contributed *to* those spikes. At best, this failure in reporting is misleading. At worst, it stokes resentment against bodies that have already borne the blame for so much, and fuels medical mistreatment of fat patients.

As covered in chapters 3 and 4, "health" was created as the antithesis of Blackness; the Black fat was always already removed from the possibility of "good" health—meaning always situated inside/under the label of "bad" health—and was to always and *already* be the criminal. From the moment white Europeans saw fat Africans, the science that followed was intended to always separate them from the rest. In this way, the BMI—created to maintain whiteness as superior—was always going to harm the Black fat and it is for this reason that Black people make up over half of the fat population and why Black people also have more "health risks" than their white counterparts.

Crack, too, is a "health" failing. The government convinced the public that Black people were the only ones doing hard drugs; that the "crackheads" were rummaging the streets looking to harm anyone who may stand in between them and their "fix"; that addiction was a moral failing rather than a direct result of one's immediate environment, overrun by poverty, anti-Blackness, and the inability to acquire proper (mental) health care. And it was this that led to punitive, carceral responses to drug addiction rather than methods rooted in harm reduction. Because the Black always already fails in, or is removed from, morality, and as such never has access to care.

The world's obsession with obesity and being overweight is less about health and is more about the cultural and systemic anti-Blackness as anti-fatness that diet, medical, and media industries profit from. Just like with the War on Drugs and the crack epidemic, major institutions falsified evidence about the effects of fatness or obesity as a way to criminalize and profit off fat people—especially the Black fat. That damage is still being done. The Black fat is not dying from being obese, nor is the Black dying from drug addiction. The Black—the Black fat—is dying because of a medical industrial complex committed to seeing fatness, Blackness, and Black fatness as death; they are dying because of a lack of proper resources—like housing and employment—that would provide them with money, health care, and a place to rest their heads; the Black fat, in particular, is dying because of an inherently anti-Black system of policing that sees them as the deadly Beast that needs to be put down. This is the Belly of the Beast: removed from care and placed always in the way of harm.

Meeting Gender's End

What has been explored throughout this book is the varying ways in which one's Blackness and fatness is always in conflict with the World; how, if one is fat and Black, they are always already illegible, animalistic, and unDesirable. This is true, too, and perhaps even more so, when one is also trans. And yet, there is so little research on fat Black trans people. It's as though we breathe in the bodies of beings that never existed. And, to some extent, we haven't and we don't. We have breath in our lungs, but existence, or who does and does not exist, is determined by people unlike us, for whom white supremacy—and more specifically, anti-Blackness—and cisheterosexism remain at the helm. But that makes trans people no less tangible. We can be physically touched, seen, and heard, and still so much about how we navigate

through and experience life is so underresearched, underval-
ued, and dismissed.

Gender, just like health and Desire/ability, is a system
forged with the purpose of creating and maintaining a
class of subjects designed to be inferior to another. The
role of "either" gender is achieved through a continued
performance. These roles—and these performances—are
implied, but also explicitly named, characteristics and
duties one must fulfill to be "man" or "woman." They are
not inherent to us, meaning we are not born as "boys" or
as "girls." In basic sociological terms, we are taught immediately after birth through social institutions like family,
media, and school what role we must fulfill if we are to
hold on to the gender we are assigned at birth. When we
start breaking the rules of those assigned roles, and thus
falling outside of gender's hold, we become "sissies" or
"tomboys"—depending on which role you were assigned to
fulfill from birth. As Judith Butler states in her book *Gender
Trouble*, our behaviors that are gendered are not innate to
us. We learn them, and then we learn to perform them.
And this performance is policed and maintained by cisheteronormativity, or the idea that everyone already is—and
therefore all things must be seen as—cisgender and heterosexual. In other words, cisheteronormativity is the "law
and order" of gender in that it is what determines who is
departing from their assigned role and must therefore be
punished because of it.

To this point, and to return to Butler, it is not our gender
that defines our performance, but rather our performance
that is always already defining our gender. In her essay,

"Performative Acts and Gender Constitution: An Essay in Phenomenology and Feminist Theory," Butler refers to gender as an illusion and an "object of belief," expanding further by noting that "gender reality is performative which means, quite simply, that it is real only to the extent that it is performed." What "performed" means in this sense is not that one is standing on a stage or pretending to do something for the sake of being lauded, but rather that one is creating the thing by which their life and beinghood is defined through myriad acts and repetitions. So what is gender? It is only what we make it, but what we make it is defined by, in simple terms, the World around us. Hortense Spillers knew this, too, about the Black, in particular, when she wrote "Mama's Baby, Papa's Maybe: An American Grammar Book." In that essay, as we covered earlier in the book, Spillers provides an analysis for what it means for Black subjects to always be "ungendered." This means that gender is lost to the Black—which more directly means that gender reads differently for our bodies and our Being. Ungendered as monstrosity—it is to suggest that we are removed from gender, that we are misaligned with a normative, "coherent" gender, making us Beasts from birth.

In summation, gender is a performance defined by our commitment to upholding it. And despite the fact that gender was never created for the Black to have access to, in similar ways to health and Desire/ability, Black subjects are socialized to uphold the violence of gender, too, and therefore can reproduce similarly violent gender restrictions. And since this is the case, gender must also be destroyed precisely because it can only ever reproduce cisheterosexist violence. And within that cisheterosexist violence, there will always also be anti-fat violence.

I spoke with seven fat Black trans people—all of whom are either trans men, transmasculine, or nonbinary—for them to tell their own stories because it's their stories that provide the data we so often lack. I asked each of them the same questions and followed up with some of them for more questioning.

The initial questions read as follows:

1. What was your journey into your trans ID like as a fat person? Has fatness played a direct role in shaping your gender journey?

2. Within Black trans/queer spaces, what type of differences do you notice between yourself and thin trans folks with regard to how you're treated?

3. More generally, how do you feel anti-fatness shows up in spaces that are predominantly trans?

The first person I spoke with was Jupiter, a nonbinary trans person who uses he/they pronouns. Jupiter had this to say:

Jupiter: *"[I] didn't know there was a word to describe how I felt, you know? Being afab, I rejected my femininity as a whole, and I find myself still doing so from time to time— even though I'm more comfortable about it than I was when I was younger, [and I was assigned] that whole 'tomboy' label. I really didn't start learning about gender identities until high school. A friend of mine, who identified as androgynous at the time, opened that door for me, but I still wasn't* *truly confident in labeling myself as trans—let alone as non-binary—[because I] still didn't understand. And yeah, I do think my fatness plays a role because I'm still pretty fucked up when it comes to my self-esteem. I find myself ping-ponging between wanting to lose weight, being happy with the way I am, or compromising and feeling like 'if I just lose a little weight in certain areas I'd be okay' because I don't really fit the nonbinary 'norm'—at least how it has been presented to me. I know not having a flat chest definitely ties into my body issues. Lately when I find myself daydreaming, I'm starting to imagine how I [could look] with a flat chest. That makes me happy, and I know that that's eventually my end goal. I haven't even attempted to invest in a binder, though, because I haven't personally seen any fat trans folx say they've found a good one that works; I'm not even sure there even* are *good binders for us.*

"I feel for sure that thin nonbinary/trans folx get more recognition and more opportunity to explore themselves and how they want to express their identity without being invalidated. It's like there are days where I don't mind being somewhat 'female-presenting,' but at the same time I'm [often] being perceived as a stud [solely] because of my body size—especially my hips. And no matter how baggy my shirt is, I can't hide my chest. So if I don't explicitly state that a spade is a spade, niggas gone say 'oh that's a diamond over there.'"

I followed up with Jupiter to ask him to say more about his feelings on wanting a flat chest. I wanted to know how he arrived at that, and if he believed that to have a flat chest meant he had to become thin.

Jupiter: *"I used to think of having a flat chest and being thin, and thought that it would make me feel good, but I'm getting better with my body image. As such, I definitely still want a flat chest, [but it doesn't have to be accompanied by a thin body]. I want a flat chest, fat body and all."*

The next person I spoke with was a transmasculine person affectionately referred to as Bearboi, with he/they pronouns.

Bearboi: *"Because people link fatness with ugliness, they think [fat folks] transition because we weren't attractive as 'women,' which isn't true, but because of the ignorance, that is what people think being trans is. Then you add the layer of being fat. I personally think that fat Black transmasc people have it extremely difficult; from the cost of transition to this idea of 'passing' being stressed because our chest size is inherently bigger than our smaller counterparts. In fact, I was actually so happy when I got a beard because there are fat cis men so I figured I could pass as one [since I had facial hair].*

"To preface this, it is not the desire [for many thin trans men] to actually be 'thin'; the goal is to be [bulky] and muscular because as a society, we associate strength and muscles with masculinity and 'manliness.' So thin transmasculine ppl do have a hard time with body image and their gender being validated because we associate being thin with femininity, and associate femininity with fragility and softness."

I explained to him that "thinness" isn't necessarily defined by who is "skinny," but rather that to be non-fat is to be thin, and as such even this societal commitment to muscularity as what "defines" manhood is still both anti-fat and cissexist. He agreed, and continued discussing weight and gym culture within trans culture:

Bearboi: *"HRT is also a big reason for this. We are told that the faster your metabolism is, the faster and better the injections work through the body. If not, it turns into estrogen and you gain weight. So many people work out to get a smaller chest area; the muscles just come with it. The smaller you can get your chest, the less you have to break your ribs wearing a binder—making pre-op more bearable. There's also the 3 stereotypical bodies people see when it comes to transmasc ppl: thin, bodybuilder, and fat. . . .*

"I don't know if you know, but top surgery for big folk is almost twice as much as it is for the thinner folk. I know someone who was quoted at $15,000 and thinner folk who were quoted at $6,500. I had a consultation at a private practice that quoted me at $9,300, I think. It was because, as they told it, legally they could not perform the surgery in their office due to my size so they would have to use the hospital and it costs more for the anesthesia. They showed me the price breakdown, and I eventually ended up going with someone else who is very familiar with working on fat bodies. There's a HUGE difference. I know some guys that were botched because their surgeon wasn't used to working on fat bodies."

I had a lot to sit with after talking to Bearboi. It was so clear to me after talking with him and Jupiter that so few thin people have interrogated gender's hold on how they view their bodies. And perhaps that is part of what allows gender to be as pervasive and as permeating as it is. How violent is it for people to determine that muscularity is required in order for one's gender to be affirmed? It seemed like the consensus was that in order for one to be trans—at least a trans person who felt happy in their body—they would have to abandon fatness, not necessarily in word but in action. I started thinking: What about those of us who are fat and don't care to be anything else? How do we create a space where a flat chest doesn't have to mean thinness or muscularity? Or a space where one doesn't have to be fixated on having a flat chest at all? Because, as I see it, a muscular chest is not flat. In fact, many men—cisgender and otherwise—refer to their muscular chests as "titties" often. So what is it about the excess fat tissue that doesn't feel affirming? Is it the way it hangs? Is it that people know, consciously or unconsciously, the harm fat people experience? Or is it that one set of non-flat chests comes with a different social status than the other?

As I pondered over it some more, I spoke to Mars, who is a nonbinary intersex person with they/them pronouns.

Mars: *"In my early to mid-20s I was seeing this white trans man. We'd been friends for a while but I'd not seen him in years. We started reconnecting and one night he took me out to a bar. I don't know if it was a date but it felt like one. All my life my gender had been questioned by others and myself but never did I have the proper term for it. Years before meeting him I found out I was intersex by resources online. It kind of shattered me because I had thought I was just some defect but then finally there was a name to it. Yet in the world I still felt like an alien. On this 'date', as I was walking into the bar, he started referring to me as she/her and they/them. It was* *new and confusing but I didn't stop him because something about it felt right. Maybe I was she/her. Maybe I was they/ them. He doesn't know it but that opened my mind a lot that night despite the confusion of our relationship and nature of his intentions.*

"Being a fat, dark-skinned, intersex queer I often put my gender and myself on the back burner. In my mind I thought nobody cared about my existence and to some extent nobody did. It was like being the most invisible but visible person because people saw my height, my skin and my fatness before they saw anything else [which meant that I had] to shrink myself in order to protect myself from the violence those three things inspired. Being fat meant I couldn't be nonbinary. Being dark-skinned meant I couldn't be queer. Most bodies I saw didn't look like mine in the world. I had to build my own space and my own lane. Experimenting with makeup and clothing, I became my own representation until I could find others like me.

"In Black queer/trans spaces, I am usually the only 'obese' person. And always the only [openly] intersex person. I'm given grace but never am I understood. I am usually simply just there to fill some quota so things look more progressive than they are. Thin trans folks usually don't see my transness because I'm fat and dark-skinned. They also don't see it because it doesn't necessarily look trans. What does looking trans mean? I'll never know, but I know it isn't what I look like according to some. In a diagram, I'm usually never in the circle; I'm usually forced to be on an island to myself.

"More generally, anti-fatness shows up in mostly all spaces because fatness is what nobody aspires to be. It's what people *aspire to run away from. In trans spaces, being fat means being the fat one and that's all you are exclusively. There's a divide because while I share transness I am not the model trans person so I will never be seen."*

After speaking with Mars, I spoke to Henry—a transmasculine person with he/him pronouns—who echoed many of the same sentiments presented by others earlier on.

Henry: *"My fatness has played a huge role in my understanding of my gender. My dysphoria was a huge part in discovering I was trans, but sometimes it was hard to separate if my discomfort was with my fatness or my gender/sex. Now that I'm secure, I can tell the difference but separating it when I didn't have the language and understanding was hard. There were also no people for me to look toward and model myself after. Being transmasc and fat, I can't think of anyone in the media that represents that. Seeing yourself in others helps with understanding and that didn't exist.*

"Perhaps the biggest difference I notice between me and thin folks is [in conversations about 'types']. Attraction is a real thing and I can't get rid of it, but as a fat person, there are very few people that I'm not attracted to. Thin folks have conversations about identity and attraction, and it basically comes down to thinness."

Jackson King, a trans man with he/him pronouns, was my follow-up to Henry. Unlike the others I had interviewed by this point, Jackson is not based in the United States. He is in London. His experiences, however, mirror those of the people mentioned above. He had this to say:

Jackson: *"I first came out as a bisexual woman. During that time, I struggled with where to place myself on the butch/ femme/androgynous woman spectrum. Of course, it turned out that I wasn't a woman after all. But one of the things that made it hard for me place myself on that butch/femme/ andro spectrum was my weight. As a fat 'woman' it often feels like androgyny (which was the thing I most identified with) is something denied to you. Androgyny is always viewed as something white, skinny and flat chested, of which I was none (I had a 38H chest). And then, in contrast, fat women must be feminine—in makeup, etc—to be celebrated and desirable. Even within fat positivity culture. And so I felt pushed into 'butchness.' I was Black. I was fat. I was masc in appearance. And it felt like that was the only space I 'fitted.' But it was something that never sat right with me. And it was a constant tension that eventually helped me realise I actually wasn't a woman after all. Instead of being a butch woman, I was actually a very camp man. So in a way, perhaps I have my fatness to thank for helping me transition. My fatness and my Blackness prevented me slotting neatly into the queer woman spectrum I was presented with. And ultimately, in time, I real- ised I didn't belong anywhere on a woman spectrum at all."*

Jackson continued by going into detail on understanding of desire and how it lives and shows up in trans spaces.

Jackson: *"I think there's a difference in perceived desire/ability [between thin trans people and fat trans people], for sure. I think another part of it for me is simply not seeing as many of us, or people who look like me. For much of my gender journey I've had to dig and search and work hard to unearth Black* *trans men who share a similar body type. Largely it feels lonely. For thin/muscular trans guys I imagine they can see themselves more reflected in Black trans culture, or in shared spaces. Whereas I constantly feel like I'm seeking people beyond Black trans culture who I can relate to in terms of fatness. In trans masc culture, the idea of being a gym bunny seems to be an unquestioned assumption. As in 'surely you're gonna go to the gym and get gains and masculinise yourself like that bro?' It feels as present in Black trans masc culture as much as the dominant white trans culture."*

I asked Jackson a few more questions, one about his experiences with medical bias and the other being a follow-up to one of his answers; I wanted him to talk more about these hegemonic masculine ideals he had described. My responses, along with my questions, read as such:

1. I hear you. It's as though the assumption is that anyone who is transmasculine in any way is always already committed to conforming to hegemonic masculinist ideals. So much so that many trans men and otherwise nonbinary masc folks feel that to be trans, they must be thin/muscular because that's the only way to affirm their gender. Even though fat trans men/nonbinary folks do exist with "breasts" or a big chest, we are most always never part of the ideal. If I'm summarizing you correctly, can you speak more to that?

2. Do you have any experiences within the medical industry where your fatness played a huge role in how your gender was engaged? For example, a lot of fat Black trans men talk about how they were quoted

rates twice as high as thin men for top surgery. I'm wondering if you have had, or know others who have, experiences like this?

Jackson: *"Oh I absolutely agree. Without top surgery and how [testosterone] has started to redistribute my body fat, I struggled a lot. Not just because of standard 'not being cisnormative' dysphoria, but because where were the transmasc folks like me? If I saw them, they were never the type that were celebrated. I feel that the assumption of seeking hegemonic masc ideals just isn't really even interrogated. Every specifically 'transmasc' space I've been in has embraced fatphobia, diet culture and gym culture as the norm. I've found it helpful to be in wider trans spaces (i.e. inclusive of trans women and nonbinary people) rather than specifically transmasc spaces for this reason. Not only have I found mainstream transmasc spaces very hegemonic in terms of [thinness], but also in terms of heterosexuality and gender expression too. It can sometimes feel like there's a silent policing of each other's masculinity.*

"[As far as medical bias], luckily I sought out a top surgeon who I knew was less fatphobic than the rest. He operates on ppl up to a BMI of 40 (many stop at 30, or occasionally 35). He also listens to what you want and delivers it—which isn't the case with all of them! Even with him though, he actively encouraged me to go on a fasting diet (the 5/2) and recommended it as he'd recently done that diet and had 'success.' I simply asked him if weight loss was a requirement for him to operate. When he said 'no but,' I was like okay then it's not happening. But I am aware of trans people who have had extremely traumatic and abusive experiences with one of the

most well-known, but also most fatphobic surgeons in the UK. It's so bad that there are large trans folks who have paid £6 to 7k for top surgery with this surgeon, only for him to leave too much breast tissue behind. Resulting in them still having dysphoria after the operation. To which this surgeon's response has been 'well it's realistic for a fat man's chest'. Some folks have literally had to pay for the procedure to be done again, with a different surgeon. For ANOTHER £7k. It's actually disgusting. And one of the more frustrating things is that a lot of the skinny transmasc folks who've had good results from this surgeon get very defensive when you point out how fatphobic and abusive this surgeon is. They say things like 'well I didn't find him inappropriate or rude' or 'I had a good experience with him' or 'he gives great results.' The lack of solidarity from skinny trans folks can be very disappointing."

After Jackson, I spoke with StoneyBertz, a nonbinary transmasculine person with they/he pronouns. Asking them the same questions I'd asked the others, StoneyBertz offered these thoughts:

StoneyBertz: *"When I was younger I was referred to as a 'tomboy,' and then growing up I was like 'oh okay, so I'm super gay,' so clinging to 'stud,' as an identifier, was a thing for a long time—mainly because I didn't know there was any other option that may have aligned with my psychology until that discovery. This is super interesting and something that I honestly think about often. I was assigned female at birth and have always been a fat person that comes from a fat family. A lot of my plans after high school were centered around losing weight and trying to join the military (which didn't happen thank the* *lord). Being a masculine-presenting, dark-skinned fat person is interesting because although I do now identify as a nonbinary trans masculine person, I honestly think that was easier for me regarding transition than other folks mainly because the identity projected onto me was always framed with those factors in mind. Like, as a dark-skinned fat 'woman' it was cool or acceptable rather for me to be masculine and present that way. I often look at my thin light-skinned counterparts and see how they often get questioned more regarding how they identify because a different idea is projected onto them. The desire/ ability politics came into play for me early on but having an understanding of those really changed how I moved after that."*

StoneyBertz is presenting something here that a few others have mentioned too. Mars talked about the difficulty of being fat and dark-skinned simultaneously, and Jackson spoke about the hardships of being unable to settle into womanhood and the general expectations of how a woman is "supposed" to perform. Dark-skinned women oftentimes have masculinity projected onto them, whereas they are masculinized in a sense, and therefore rejected access to femininity and, thus, desire. Light-skinned women, on the contrary, are expected to be feminine. Much of their social currency and Desire Capital is predicated on their ability to perform their gender in a way that is aligned with the social expectations of what femininity should and should not look like. StoneyBertz is speaking to this phenomenon here when they talk about the ways in which their gender performance, at the time, was policed in a different way than that of their light-skinned peers.

They continue by talking more about Desire/ability, specifically in trans spaces.

StoneyBertz: *"[In trans spaces], I usually experience a major difference in access, a lot of which is aided by the other systems designed to oppress like the racist healthcare system in addition to what is expected in these spaces. When fat folks show up to be a part of an open mic of a conversation regarding self-love or the like, it is always an observation for me that discussions of fatphobia on its face is almost impossible. It's almost as if being welcomed into those spaces is contingent on speaking only about shared trauma as opposed to other factors like colorism and fatphobia which also plague us. It just seems infinitely harder to get to the meat of things when this is the case in these spaces. I think [these differences] show up in how we talk about bodies in general. There are always campaigns for support for binders or gender affirming surgeries, but often I think we ignore the reality for fat folks. I had to go to a certain company for a binder that was big enough and comfortable for me. In order to have top surgery, my BMI has to be 35 or lower. We like to proselytize about embracing our different bodies and valuing everyone, but these conversations are based [on thin people unless they decide] to center or make room for fat folks rather. Even the way folks interact with you, they almost don't expect you to care about yourself in the same way or have the same interest in how you present because they project this attitude that because you are fat that you are happy with [just being tolerated] in the space rather than centered there."*

Finally, I wrapped up my interviews with Micah A, a trans man with they/he pronouns.

Micah A: *"I had never thought about fatness, my fat body specifically, in relation to transness. I knew that it was prevalent before transitioning and coming out as queer, but never thought about the ways it has shaped or directed my journey. I also believe as I change and navigate queer communities, the way my body is read and/or perceived changes based on desire individually but also as a community. Our desires usually aren't our own. They're shaped socially. I don't think I had time to nurture or create a space for my fatness. I was too busy picking apart my body in other ways. And maybe that's because the world didn't pay attention to it. Or in my head, it was more about 'passing' and hiding away the most ethnic pieces of me, pointing more to my trans body and my very Black features. Also, being masculine-presenting my entire life shaped the ways in which the world saw me. Fatness attached to masculine bodies and/or men is perceived differently than fatness attached to feminine bodies and/or women.*

"Being masculine-presenting allowed me to 'escape' fatphobia in ways that feminine presenting folks aren't able to. And this doesn't mean I don't experience it, it's just executed differently. I spent most of my life inside of lesbian spaces, and it wasn't until I began to add cismen, specifically, into my space that I noticed the outward fatphobia. Gay men made it clear that they would not sleep with or date fat men, [and that became an example of the more forward fatphobia I would have to endure].

"It's difficult finding trans community, Black trans community specifically. A few weeks ago, there was this conversation on twitter about white trans men using #TransmanThirstdae. A white trans man posted his pics and [the tweet] went viral, but the hashtag was made for Black trans men to have a space to exist and feel great in our skin. White trans men have enough space. His picture going viral, in ways that Black trans men have never experienced, highlighted our understanding and perceptions of beauty as we navigate transness. And I thought, 'but what would this look like if we centered Black, dark-skinned, fat trans men? Would we show up in numbers how we did today? Are the Black trans men going viral on Twitter fat? They usually are light-skinned and skinny. Why do we continue to uphold and maintain this very restricted idea of beauty while already being marginalized?'"

None of the people who provided testimonials for this chapter had spoken to any other participant before answering my questions, and yet each of them provided similar responses to each other. That is not coincidental. Fat Black trans people are forced to move to and through gender in a way that makes most evident to me that gender itself is something worth interrogating more closely. In so many ways, fatness functions as a gender of its own. Fatness fails, and therefore disrupts, the foundation on which gender is built. This is why the request is made of fat trans people to lose weight before they can be affirmed in their gender, or why little fat Black boys are often misread as girls, or why fat Black women are often denied access to womanhood in a way that operates differently than the typical ungendering

of Black subjects at large. But gender is birthed from violence, and therefore fatness operating as its own gender is
not liberatory so much as it is forced. Fat people are situated in this extension of what is already a prison because fat
bodies deviate from—or rather are already positioned outside of—the designated or assigned "look" of gender. This
is to say that the attempt to broaden the normate template
only further harms unDesirable people and reifies the very
real violences of gender itself.[1]

At the beginning of this chapter, we defined gender. What
the seven subjects walked us through after that is something
we also agreed on at the start of the chapter: gender is only
what we make it. All seven of them, in one way or another,
talked about how much they had to almost force themselves
into a space; how they had to forge their own paths, create
their own gender within a gender, because their fatness had
already denied them the ability to do anything but that.
They each also presented this truth, even if unknowingly
so: in so many ways, gender is defined by thinness in that
for one to "fit comfortably" into the performance, they must
always be pushing away from fatness to not otherwise be
engaged as the Beast. If shedding oneself of fatness, or altogether removing themselves from fat as an identity, is the
only way for one's gender to be affirmed—both socially and
surgically—perhaps gender is no longer a performance we
can afford to keep in business.

Fat trans people are finding it nearly impossible to find
binders that feel affirming for them; many are being forced to
engage an inherently anti-Black and anti-fat medical system
that uses body mass index as an indicator for whether or

not they deserve to be affirmed in their bodies; we are being engaged as the Other, even in spaces that, in name, were created for our comfort and safety. Gender works in relationship to health and Desire as a means to further ostracize the Black fat, and as this is the case, only one solution will prove to be sufficient enough for our liberation: we must see to gender's end, which means we must destroy gender.

Beyond Abolition

Throughout this book, I have hinted at in some places, and named explicitly in others, the need to move beyond. In the introduction, I wrote about the need to move beyond self-love, even a self-love that is radical. In the chapters that followed, I wrote about the need to move beyond health as a qualifier for the Black fat; I wrote about the need to move beyond Desire/ability, the need to move beyond the Human, or rather the need to move beyond the desire to be Human and the need to move beyond gender. In chapter 4, I offered something that, depending on where your politic is as you read this book, may have been more radical than the other ideas presented: the need to move beyond abolition. Beyond prison abolition, beyond the abolition of police, beyond the abolition of slavery. In recent years, the idea of abolition has become increasingly more popular. The ideology itself, however, is not new. Black feminist thinkers and abolitionist scholars like Ruth Wilson Gilmore, Angela Y. Davis, Mariame Kaba, and many others have done necessary, groundbreaking work within this particular field to provide a blueprint of sorts for what life can look like if abolition is made possible.

At its core, abolition is not just the closing of jails, disbanding of prisons, and the undoing of institutionalized policing, it is also intended to introduce necessary resources into communities that so often lack those resources. For example, one reason for defunding police could be to allocate those additional funds to education programs, or to fund affordable housing and shelters for folks without homes. Similarly, one reason to close a jail could be to allocate the funds intended to be put toward a jail during a city's fiscal year toward building a community center in its place—increasing employment opportunities, providing more direct access to mental health services, creating after-school programs, and more. As abolitionists, that is part of the work we do. Abolitionists also create the necessary language and environments to move our particular communities away from punitive and carceral responses to harm and abuse, introducing ways to deal with these issues through restorative and transformative measures. As such, abolitionists don't ask, "How do we deal with abusers?" and instead ask, "How can we better the conditions of the communities most often impacted by police, prisons, and other forms of state violence so that they have the resources to not need or desire to commit this harm?" Meaning that, at the heart of it, abolitionists are focused on harm prevention *as well as* harm reduction. With this in mind, however, abolition is so often spoken about as though it is the end. If we abolish police, if we abolish prisons, if we abolish the criminal justice system, then the violence of the institutions themselves will be undone.

What is rarely ever examined, though, is that systems and institutions are maintained by power but are created first through an idea. At the root, liberation must mean cultural revolution as well as a destruction of the sociopolitical institutions that hold these systems in place, which means that abolition cannot be the end; it must only be the beginning. As we discussed earlier in the book, the end goal must be a complete destruction of the World itself—whereby I mean that the World only exists because anti-Black, capitalist, cis-heteropatriarchal systems of violence and domination exist and therefore must, itself, be destroyed. Systems are built by an idea and the power to actualize the idea, which means that if abolition is only about eradicating systems or providing resources to people within the World through which those systems are created, it cannot be and is not enough. In other words, the World gives birth to and incubates these institutions; it is not created by them.

Think about it: before policing was institutionalized, there were people so committed to seeing Black subjects only ever as property that they were willing to kill for it. The idea of a slave patrol was actualized before the first police force in the North was ever institutionalized—which came long before the first institutionalized police force in the South. The Thirteenth Amendment, passed and ratified by Congress in 1865, abolished slavery in the United States, and yet the Black is still disproportionately locked in cages, trapped by chains, and forced to perform labor for no more than a nickel and a dime. And as Strings notes in *Fearing the Black Body*, anti-fatness had already been an idea circulating before it was formed into a coherent ideology made possible through colonialism, Christianity, and anti-Blackness.

At the nucleus of all of these violent structures is anti-Blackness, on which the World is built. This means that unless and until we are committed first and always to destroying anti-Blackness, these institutions will always find a way to reinvent themselves. After reading this, some of you may ask, "So what comes after we destroy the World?" And my answer is that that's not a question I can answer alone. Individuals don't create new realities alone. As Ruth Wilson Gilmore states in *Golden Gulag: Prisons, Surplus, Crisis, and Opposition in Globalizing California*, "if it takes a village to raise a child, it certainly takes a movement to undo an occupation." And if it takes a movement to undo an occupation, it certainly takes a community to build a new reality. What I am certain of is this: what happens beyond can't be answered until the Beyond is here. What we do know is that this—the World—can no longer exist. From its inception, the World has sought to kill the Black fat. And it has been successful. Through the institutionalization of health, gender, policing, and Desire—ideas made manifest by power—the Black fat has suffered. Abolition, then, must only be the start. If it is the end, as we have seen already, the Black fat will continue to suffer.

In *Hunger: A Memoir of (My) Body*, Roxane Gay refers to her body as a "cage" of her own making; one that she has been trying to figure a way out of for more than twenty years. I see the Black fat body not as a cage, but rather as a thing that has been caged. A thing, a Beast, bound by the structures of the World. And so, then, I echo and employ the words of the late Maya Angelou who wrote of why the caged bird sings. If that caged bird is the Beast, trapped and taunted by the idea of freedom, then like it, the Black fat sings with a fearful trill of things unknown but longed for still; we sit on graves of dreams not yet seen. In those dreams, which may never resurrect, there's a place—not the World—where we live and breathe as beings not bound by identifiers and qualifiers predicated on anti-Blackness. Where we are not Black or white, not thin or fat, not cis or trans, not queer or straight, not bound or unbound. In that place, the caged bird is not freed from its cage; in that place, the cage never existed for the bird to ever be bound by.

Moving beyond abolition requires that we destroy the World that produces the cage by which the Black fat is bound.

NOTES

Chapter 2

1. Janet Mock, "Being Pretty Is a Privilege, but We Refuse to Acknowledge It," *Allure*, June 28, 2017, www.allure.com/story/pretty-privilege.

2. Frank B. Wilderson III, "Unspeakable Ethics," in *Red, White & Black: Cinema and the Structure of U.S. Antagonisms* (Durham: Duke University Press, 2010), 1–35.

3. bell hooks, "Understanding Patriarchy," 2010, https://imaginenoborders.org/pdf/zines/Understanding Patriarchy.pdf.

4. Heather Laine Talley, *Saving Face: Disfigurement and the Politics of Appearance*, (New York: NYU Press, 2014), 76.

5. Stuart W. Flint, et al., "Obesity Discrimination in the Recruitment Process: 'You're Not Hired!,'" *Frontiers in Psychology* 7, no. 647 (May 3, 2016), https://doi.org/10.3389/fpsyg.2016.00647.

6. Areva Martin, "49 States Legally Allow Employers to Discriminate Based on Weight," *Time*, August 16, 2017, https://time.com/4883176/weight-discrimination-workplace-laws.

7. Jack Tsai and Robert A. Rosenheck, "Obesity among
Chronically Homeless Adults: Is It a Problem?" *Public
Health Reports* 128, no. 1 (2013): 29–36, https://doi.org
/10.1177/003335491312800105.

8. Your Fat Friend, "Why Don't We Hear Fat Women's
#MeToo Stories?" *Medium*, August 15, 2018, https://
medium.com/the-establishment/why-dont-we-hear
-fat-women-s-metoo-stories-2e28f799b507?source
=linkShare-61dcd8dfa08-1567785399.

9. Your Fat Friend, "How Health Care Bias Harms Fat
Patients," *Medium*, January 16, 2019, https://medium.com
/@thefatshadow/the-bias-epidemic-8f27e79bd21c?source
=linkShare-61dcd8dfa08-156778544.

10. Aisha Harris, "Was There Really 'Mandingo Fighting,'
Like in *Django Unchained*?," *Slate*, December 24, 2012,
https://slate.com/culture/2012/12/django-unchained
-mandingo-fighting-were-any-slaves-really-forced-to
-fight-each-other-to-the-death.html.

11. hooks, "Understanding Patriarchy."

12. Milo W. Obourn, *Disabled Futures: A Framework for Radical Inclusion* (Philadelphia: Temple University Press,
2020).

13. Jessie W. Parkhurst, "The Role of the Black Mammy in
the Plantation Household," *The Journal of Negro History*
23, no. 3 (1938): 349–69, https://https://doi.org/10.2307
/2714687.

Chapter 3

1. Preamble to the Constitution of WHO as adopted by the
International Health Conference, New York, 19 June–22

July 1946; signed on 22 July 1946 by the representatives of 61 States (Official Records of WHO, no. 2, p. 100) and entered into force on 7 April 1948.

2. J. F. Blumenbach, *On the Natural Variety of Mankind,* third ed. 1795, in *The Anthropological Treatises of Johann Friedrich Blumenbach,* trans. Thomas Bendyshe (London: Longman, Green, Longman, Roberts, and Green, 1865), 145–276.

3. James Denny Guillory, "The Pro-Slavery Arguments of Dr. Samuel A. Cartwright," *Louisiana History: The Journal of the Louisiana Historical Association* 9, no. 3 (1968): 209–27, www.jstor.org/stable/4231017.

4. "Teen's Death at Camp Fuels Debate, Inquiry," *Los Angeles Times,* December 5, 1999, www.latimes.com/archives /la-xpm-1999-dec-05-mn-40755-story.html.

5. Paul R. La Monica, "Weight Watchers Is Changing Its Name to WW," *CNN Money,* 2018, https://money.cnn .com/2018/09/24/news/companies/weight-watchers-new -name-ww/index.html.

6. Virgie Tovar, "Dear Virgie: What's the History of Diet Culture?," *Wear Your Voice,* February 24, 2016, https:// wearyourvoicemag.com/dear-virgie-whats-history-diet -culture/.

7. Harriet Brown, "The Weight of the Evidence," *Slate,* March 24, 2015, https://slate.com/technology/2015/03 /diets-do-not-work-the-thin-evidence-that-losing -weight-makes-you-healthier.html.

8. Peter Rzehak et al., "Weight Change, Weight Cycling and Mortality in the ERFORT Male Cohort Study," *European Journal of Epidemiology* 22, no. 10 (August 4, 2007): 665– 673, https://pubmed.ncbi.nlm.nih.gov/17676383/.

9. American Heart Association, "Yo-Yo Dieting May Increase Women's Heart Disease Risk," *ScienceDaily*, www.sciencedaily.com/releases/2019/03/190307161902.htm.

10. bell hooks, "Understanding Patriarchy," 2010, https:// imaginenoborders.org/pdf/zines/Understanding Patriarchy.pdf.

11. Adee Braun, "Looking to Quell Sexual Urges? Consider the Graham Cracker," *The Atlantic*, January 15, 2014, www. theatlantic.com/health/archive/2014/01/looking-to-quell-sexual-urges-consider-the-graham-cracker/282769/.

Chapter 4

1. Al Baker, J. David Goodman, and Benjamin Mueller, "Beyond the Chokehold: The Path to Eric Garner's Death," *New York Times*, June 13, 2015, www.nytimes.com /2015/06/14/nyregion/eric-garner-police-chokehold -staten-island.html.

2. Mike Lillis, "Pete King: Garner's Obesity, Medical Condition Led to Death," *The Hill*, December 4, 2014, https:// thehill.com/blogs/blog-briefing-room/news/225956 -peter-king-blame-garners-obesity-medical-condition -for-death.

3. Associated Press, "Medical Examiner: Chokehold Triggered Eric Garner's Death," *Fox News*, May 15, 2019, www.foxnews.com/us/medical-examiner-chokehold -triggered-eric-garners-death.

4. Associated Press, "Chokehold Triggered Eric Garner's Death."

5. Baker, Goodman, and Mueller, "Beyond the Chokehold."

6. Sherronda J. Brown, "Within a White Supremacist System, Eric Garner's True Crime Was Being Fat," *Wear Your Voice*, June 17, 2019, https://wearyourvoicemag.com/eric-garner-fatphobia/.

7. Jamelle Bouie, "Michael Brown Wasn't a Superhuman Demon to Anyone but Darren Wilson," *Slate*, November 26, 2014, https://slate.com/news-and-politics/2014/11/darren-wilsons-racial-portrayal-of-michael-brown-as-a-superhuman-demon-the-ferguson-police-officers-account-is-a-common-projection-of-racial-fears.html.

8. Krishnadev Calamur, "Ferguson Documents: Officer Darren Wilson's Testimony," *NPR*, November 25, 2014, www.npr.org/sections/thetwo-way/2014/11/25/366519644/ferguson-docs-officer-darren-wilsons-testimony.

9. Damien Cave, "Officer Darren Wilson's Grand Jury Testimony in Ferguson, Mo., Shooting," *New York Times*, November 25, 2014, www.nytimes.com/interactive/2014/11/25/us/darren-wilson-testimony-ferguson-shooting.html.

10. Bouie, "Michael Brown Wasn't a Superhuman Demon."

11. Eric Heisig, "A Breakdown of the Events That Led to the 12-Year-Old's Death," *Cleveland.com*, January 14, 2017, www.cleveland.com/court-justice/2017/01/tamir_rice_shooting_a_breakdow.html.

12. Cory Shaffer, "9-1-1 Caller Says Gun Held by Cleveland 12-Year-Old Shot by Police Was 'Probably Fake,'" November 23, 2014, www.cleveland.com/metro/2014/11/9-1-1_caller_says_gun_held_by.html.

13. DiversityInc Staff, "Tamir Rice's Age, Size Repeatedly Made an Issue in Shooting Investigation," *DiversityInc*,

January 11, 2019, www.diversityinc.com/tamir-rices
-age-size-repeatedly-made-an-issue-in-shooting
-investigation/.

14. Harriet McLeod, "South Carolina Cop Staged Scene
after Shooting Black Man: Prosecutor," *Reuters*, November 3, 2016, www.reuters.com/article/us-south-carolina
-shooting-slager-idUSKBN12Y1XU.

15. "The Shooting of Samuel DuBose," *Harvard Law
Review*, February 10, 2016, https://harvardlawreview.org
/2016/02/the-shooting-of-samuel-dubose/.

16. Alex Johnson and Gabe Gutierrez, "Baton Rouge Store
Owner Says His Video Shows Cops 'Murdered' Alton
Sterling," *NBC News*, July 7, 2016, www.nbcnews.com
/news/us-news/baton-rouge-store-owner-says-his-video
-shows-cops-murdered-n604841.

17. Jim Mustian and Lea Skene, "New Alton Sterling Shooting Videos Show Deadly, Heated Scene at Triple S," *The
Advocate*, March 30, 2018, www.theadvocate.com
/baton_rouge/news/alton_sterling/article_209c1f62-33c7
-11e8-a2c8-179ff7c92a3f.html.

18. BBC Staff, "George Floyd: What Happened in the Final
Moments of His Life," *BBC*, July 16, 2020, www.bbc.com
/news/world-us-canada-52861726.

19. Eric Levenson, "Former Officer Knelt on George Floyd
for 9 Minutes and 29 Seconds—Not the Infamous 8:46,"
CNN, March 30, 2021, https://www.cnn.com/2021/03/29
/us/george-floyd-timing-929-846/index.html.

20. Charlie Wiese, "Autopsy Report: George Floyd Died
from Cardiopulmonary Arrest, Was Positive for

COVID-19," June 3, 2020, https://kstp.com/news/george
-floyd-autopsy-report-shows-george-floyd-died-from
-cardiopulmonary-arrest-was-positive-for-covid-19
/5750262/.

21. Lorenzo Reyes, Trevor Hughes, and Mark Emmert, "Medical Examiner and Family-Commissioned Autopsy Agree: George Floyd's Death Was a Homicide," *USA Today*, June 2, 2020, www.usatoday.com/story/news/nation/2020/06/01/george-floyd-independent-autopsy-findings-released-monday/5307185002/.

22. Cheryl I. Harris, "Whiteness as Property," *Harvard Law Review*, June 10, 1993, https://harvardlawreview.org/1993/06/whiteness-as-property/.

23. Josh Sanburn, "All the Ways Darren Wilson Described Being Afraid of Michael Brown," *Time*, November 25, 2014, https://time.com/3605346/darren-wilson-michael-brown-demon/.

Chapter 5

1. "Defining Adult Overweight and Obesity," Centers for Disease Control and Prevention, September 17, 2020, www.cdc.gov/obesity/adult/defining.html.

2. Eliot Marshall, "Public Enemy Number One: Tobacco or Obesity?" *Science* 304, no. 5672 (May 7, 2004): 804, https://doi.org/10.1126/science.304.5672.804.

3. Betsy McKay, "CDC Study Overstated Obesity as a Cause of Death," *Wall Street Journal*, November 23, 2004, www.wsj.com/articles/SB110117970881981681.

4. McKay, "CDC Study."

5. Gina Kolata, "Why Do Obese Patients Get Worse Care? Many Doctors Don't See Past the Fat," *New York Times*, September 26, 2016, www.nytimes.com/2016/09/26/health /obese-patients-health-care.html.

6. McKay, "CDC Study."

7. Rosie Mestel, "Disputed Obesity Study Slipped through CDC Filters," *Los Angeles Times*, February 10, 2005, www.latimes.com/archives/la-xpm-2005-feb-10-sci -obese10-story.html.

8. The Center for Consumer Freedom Team, "New JAMA Study Challenges CDC's 400,000 Obesity Deaths Figure," Center for Consumer Freedom, April 19, 2005, www.consumerfreedom.com/press-releases/99-new -jama-study-challenges-cdcs-400000-obesity-deaths -figure/.

9. Ed Vulliamy, "Nixon's 'War on Drugs' Began 40 Years Ago, and the Battle Is Still Raging," *The Guardian*, July 23, 2011, www.theguardian.com/society/2011/jul/24/war-on -drugs-40-years.

10. Michael Kunzelman, Dylan Lovan, and Adrian Sainz, "Deadly Police Raid Fuels Call to End 'No Knock' War- rants," *Seattle Times*, May 31, 2020, www.seattletimes .com/nation-world/nation/deadly-police-raid-fuels-call -to-end-no-knock-warrants/.

11. Kenneth B. Nunn, "Race, Crime and the Pool of Surplus Criminality: Or Why the 'War on Drugs' Was a 'War on Blacks,'" 2002, https://scholarship.law.ufl.edu /facultypub/107/.

12. "A Brief History of the Drug War," Drug Policy Alliance, www.drugpolicy.org/issues/brief-history-drug-war.

13. Drug Policy Alliance, "A Brief History."
14. Drug Policy Alliance, "A Brief History."
15. Tim Naftali, "Ronald Reagan's Long-Hidden Racist Conversation with Richard Nixon," *The Atlantic*, July 31, 2019, www.theatlantic.com/ideas/archive/2019/07/ronald -reagans-racist-conversation-richard-nixon/595102/.
16. Erna Kubergovic, "Quetelet, Adolphe," Eugenics Archive, 2013, http://eugenicsarchive.ca/discover/tree /5233cb0f5c2ec5000000009c.
17. Aubrey Gordon, "The Bizarre and Racist History of the BMI," *Elemental*, October 15, 2019, https://elemental .medium.com/the-bizarre-and-racist-history-of-the -bmi-7d8dc2aa33bb.

Chapter 6

1. Rosemarie Garland-Thomson, "Integrating Disability, Transforming Feminist Theory," *NWSA Journal* 14, no. 3 (2002): 1–32, https://doi.org/10.2979/nws.2002.14.3.1.

REFERENCES

Angelou, Maya. *Shaker, Why Don't You Sing?* New York: Random House, 1983.

Athanassoglou-Kallmyer, Nina. "Ugliness." In *On the Politics of Ugliness*, 31–50. London: Palgrave Macmillan, 2018.

Butler, Judith. *Gender Trouble: Feminism and the Subversion of Identity.* New York: Routledge, 1990.

Butler, Judith. "Performative Acts and Gender Constitution: An Essay in Phenomenology and Feminist Theory." *Theatre Journal* 40, no. 4 (1988): 519–31. https://doi.org/10.2307/3207893.

Davis, Angela Y. *Are Prisons Obsolete?* New York: Seven Stories Press, 2003.

Foucault, Michel. *Discipline and Punish: The Birth of the Prison.* Translated by Alan Sheridan. New York: Vintage Books, 1977.

Gay, Roxane. *Hunger: A Memoir of (My) Body.* New York: HarperCollins, 2017.

Gilmore, Ruth Wilson. *Golden Gulag: Prisons, Surplus, Crisis, and Opposition in Globalizing California.* Berkeley: University of California Press, 2006.

Goff, Phillip Atiba, et al. "The Essence of Innocence: Consequences of Dehumanizing Black Children." *Journal of Personality and Social Psychology* 106, no. 4 (April 2014): 526–45. https://doi.org/10.1037/a0035663.

Gonzalez Van Cleve, Nicole. *Crook County: Racism and Injustice in America's Largest Criminal Court*. Stanford: Stanford University Press, 2017.

Hartman, Saidiya V. *Scenes of Subjection: Terror, Slavery, and Self-Making in Nineteenth-Century America*. New York: Oxford University Press, 1997.

Jackson, Zakiyyah Iman. "Animality and Blackness." *Genealogy of the Posthuman*. September 29, 2020. https://criticalposthumanism.net/animality-and-blackness/.

Jackson, Zakiyyah Iman. *Becoming Human: Matter and Meaning in an Antiblack World*. New York: New York University Press, 2020.

Laymon, Kiese. *Heavy: An American Memoir*. New York: Scribner, 2019.

Obourn, Milo W. *Disabled Futures: A Framework for Radical Inclusion*. Philadelphia: Temple University Press, 2020.

Oliver, J. Eric. *Fat Politics: The Real Story behind America's Obesity Epidemic*. New York: Oxford University Press, 2006.

Przybylo, Ela, and Sara Rodrigues, eds. *On the Politics of Ugliness*. London: Palgrave Macmillan, 2018.

Spillers, Hortense J. "Mama's Baby, Papa's Maybe: An American Grammar Book." In *Black, White, and in Color: Essays on American Literature and Culture*, 203–29. Chicago: The University of Chicago Press, 2003.

Strings, Sabrina. *Fearing the Black Body: The Racial Origins of Fat Phobia*. New York: New York University Press, 2019.

Talley, Heather Laine. *Saving Face: Disfigurement and the Politics of Appearance*. New York: New York University Press, 2014.

Taylor, Sonia Renee. *The Body Is Not an Apology: The Power of Radical Self-Love*. Oakland, CA: Berrett-Koehler Publishers, 2018.

Turner, K. B., David Giacopassi, and Margaret Vandiver. "Ignoring the Past: Coverage of Slavery and Slave Patrols in Criminal Justice Texts." *Journal of Criminal Justice Education* 17, no. 1 (2007): 181–195. https://doi.org/10.1080/10511250500335627.

Wilderson III, Frank. *Red, White & Black: Cinema and the Structure of U.S. Antagonisms*. Durham, NC: Duke University Press, 2010.

INDEX

ABOUT THE AUTHOR

Da'Shaun L. Harrison is a Black, fat, disabled, queer, and trans writer. They are also an abolitionist and community organizer based in Atlanta, Georgia. Harrison has worn, and continues to wear, many hats: communications director, editor in chief, associate editor, managing editor, lead organizer, and now author.

Harrison travels throughout the United States and abroad to lecture at conferences and colleges, and to lead workshops focused on Blackness, queerness, gender, class, (dis)abilities, fatness, and the intersection at which they all meet. You can find Da'Shaun on Twitter and Instagram @DaShaunLH, or through their website, dashaunharrison.com.

About North Atlantic Books

North Atlantic Books (NAB) is a 501(c)(3) nonprofit publisher committed to a bold exploration of the relationships between mind, body, spirit, culture, and nature. Founded in 1974, NAB aims to nurture a holistic view of the arts, sciences, humanities, and healing. To make a donation or to learn more about our books, authors, events, and newsletter, please visit www.northatlanticbooks.com.